I Declare Before My God

The True Story of a Father and Son,
Brian and James Seery

Brian executed in Ireland, 13 February 1846

James executed in Australia, 14 November 1870

I DECLARE BEFORE MY GOD

The Brian and James Seery Story

Jack Kiernan

First published in 2019 by The Manuscript Publisher

ISBN: 978-1-911442-11-0

A CIP Catalogue record for this book is available from the National Library

Typesetting, page design and layout, cover design by DocumentsandManuscripts.com based on photos and illustrations used courtesy of Jack Kiernan, Dave Charleston (*Gippsland in Pictures*) and National Archives, Bishop Street, Dublin

Published, printed and bound in Ireland

I Declare Before My God

Copyright © Jack Kiernan, 2019

Dedication

To my late parents, Seán and Iris

In Memoriam

To the memory of all innocent men and women put to death by the British authorities, especially, father and son, Brian and James Seery, two innocent Irishmen murdered by the British Ascendency.

Brian was executed/murdered in Ireland on Friday, 13 February 1846. Twenty-four years and nine months later, James suffered a similar fate, also at the hands of the British. James was executed/murdered in Australia on 14 November 1870. He was 33 years of age.

Also, to the memory of a wife and mother, Mary Seery. This young lady was left on her own to bring up five young children through very difficult times.

What They Said

Daniel O'Connell, MP during Question Time in the House of Commons asked:

Whether a deputation consisting of several persons waited on His Excellency, the Lord Lieutenant, after the conviction and before the execution of Brian Seery, to pray that the convict should not be respited or, his sentence transmuted but, that he should be executed?

O'Connell went on to mention a similar case, in which he had been counsel, when

Chief Justice Pennefather ruled that his (O'Connell's) argument was inconsistent with the practice and the trial was proceeded with. The twelve judges met on the subject and though they gave no decision, it was understood they had formed an opinion adverse to that of Chief Justice Pennefather.

Charles Dickens, Author

Dickens was well known for his views on Capital Punishment. In a letter to the Daily News he asked:

Whether the death penalty encouraged repentance and reform and whether fallible human beings were justified in imposing such an irrevocable punishment?

He cited the recent case of Irishman, Brian Seery, who, he said,

... had been executed for attempting to murder his former landlord, despite extremely questionable evidence and his own persistent protestations of innocence.

Adding,

...the barest possibility of mistake is sufficient reason against taking a life which nothing can restore.

Most Rev Dr Cantwell, Bishop of Meath

The manner in which the commission was obtained and carried out; the unimpeached excellence of Seery's character through life; the omission to summon Catholic jurors; the sectarian arrangement of the

general list; the dissent of the jury on the first trial; the exclusion by the Crown of respectable gentlemen on the second trial to which the Crown resorted after the trifling of a day from the discharge of the first jury.

The jury, not having given weight to the testimony of the stipendiary magistrate, of two policemen and of six other credible and respectable witnesses, all contradicting the evidence given by the prosecutor (Hopkins), who, in a most important fact, contradicted even himself.

The public are impressed with the belief that the magistrates of the county (with some few honourable exceptions) and the local officials who have for years enforced an anti-Catholic bitterness unknown in other parts of Ireland, have, in this instance, done everything in their power to secure a victim. The people feel that vengeance and not justice has been, with a certain class, a leading object.

Fr Savage, Chaplain Mullingar Gaol

Sir Francis is annoyed at the comments that have been made by the press on the contradiction between the testimony of Mr French, the stipendiary magistrate and his own. He tells us that he has letters from a policeman and an attorney's clerk to prove that he himself was right and then, in triumph, he concludes by saying, the public can now fairly judge between Mr French's testimony and my own.

How a drowning man clutches at reeds!

I wish the baronet may attempt an explanation in his next letter of the contradiction between Sir Francis Hopkins on the first trial and Sir Francis Hopkins on the second. Will the police or the attorney's clerk stand to him on this point?

The Tablet

If the facts be truly reported and really, there seems to be no difference of opinion on this point, we have no hesitation in saying that, if it be murder to employ against a man an instrument or means which are sure to bring about his death, whether he be innocent or guilty, then Brian Seery is a murdered man.

Evening Mail

A conspiracy is raging in Ireland, possessing all the characteristics of a civil war of population against property, of creed against religion. It is a war of Papists against Protestants, the confederates or conspirators being exclusively Roman Catholics and bound by a terrible oath to exterminate, even by death, the professors of the creed opposed to them. This is the Ribbon obligation, described and denounced by Lord Plunkett. We repeat that no Roman Catholic should sit on a jury.

Crown Solicitor – Mr S. Seed

Prior to Brian Seery's second trial, Mr Seed, Crown Solicitor included the following sentence in a letter to Dublin Castle:

I beg to state that I have had an opportunity of conversing with many of the Grand Jurors at present assembled here on the subject of the Commission and they all seem to be very well satisfied, and I think it will very probably be the means of restoring tranquillity to the County.

Chief Justice Doherty

I have seldom had cases brought before me – cases which more exhibited the dreadful scourge that, wherever it was permitted to take root, struck at the very foundation of all social order and placed in jeopardy the peace and security of every individual in the country.

Sir Francis Hopkins – Alleged Victim

Prior to Brian Seery's arrest, a man he knew very well, Hopkins, made a statement, which he read and signed. It contained the following:

I was attacked by two unknown assailants; I would recognise one of them if I saw him again.

After Seery's arrest, Hopkins asked to make a second statement. This statement contained the following:

I was attacked by Brian Seery and another assailant.

Brian Seery – The Real Victim

Prior to his execution Seery issued the following statement from his cell:

I, Brian Seery, now a prisoner in the gaol in Mullingar and on this day to be executed, do most solemnly and sincerely declare, in the presence of that God before whom I must shortly appear for judgement, that I never fired at Sir Francis Hopkins, that I never committed any act tending to injure him in person or property and that I was never cognizant of, or a party to any conspiracy to plot or shoot or injure the said Sir Francis Hopkins, and that I am not guilty, directly or indirectly, of the crime for which I am to be hanged.

Later, when Seery stood on the gallows, while raising his crucifix, he said in a calm, loud and steady tone, with an emphasis of awful and terrible solemnity:

I declare before my God that I had neither act, hand, part or knowledge in the crime for which I am going to die here!

Dr Ferguson (treated Hopkins after the incident)

On the 17 February, (a few days after Seery's execution), Ferguson wrote to Sir Francis Hopkins and mentioned the following:

The odium of hanging Seery being exclusively on you and me and, perhaps, equally as much on the police for "paid swearing" but, as it is said, "their evidence not being believed", that we are the persons who hung him.

Note

During the proceedings, the British judiciary and media spelt Brian with a "y" (Bryan). However, according to his family headstone Brian is the correct spelling.

Preface

Throughout this story, I mention the British, Brits and English, however, I don't mean the ordinary British/English man or woman on the street. I am referring to the Ascendency, Gentry etc. These people also terrorised their unfortunate fellow countrymen and women. The poor and vulnerable English suffered the same fate as the poor in Ireland. They were subjected to the hangman's rope or transportation to faraway places, just like the Irish, Scots and Welsh.

We only need to go back as far as the Great War and the "Shot at Dawn" murders to realise the type of people the British Aristocracy were. These people made no bones about killing their own soldiers – brave young men from all over these islands.

Nearer home, there was the Castlepollard Massacre: on 23 May 1831. Thirteen civilians were massacred by RIC officers. Among the dead were three ladies; many more were injured.

Dublin, 29 April 1916: The British shot and stabbed innocent civilians to death. Among the victims – fourteen in all – were 16-year-old Christopher Hickey and his father Thomas. The victims were killed in what became known as the "North King Street Massacre". Some of these innocent people were dragged from their homes, others from their place of employment. Young Christopher Hickey's case proved, beyond a shadow of a doubt, that as far as the British were concerned, Irish children were fair game.

The Croke Park killings of 21 November 1920 were another example of their murderous mentality, they opened fire on innocent people in the presence of thousands of witnesses. They just did not care.

It is a known fact that natives in every country colonised by the British suffered atrocities at the hands of their sinister conquerors. Murder, rape, destruction, skulduggery, skulthuggery, skulmuggery, and even skulbuggery were all part and parcel of their modus operandi. They introduced nothing but hardship to their unfortunate victims as they plundered their way through foreign lands. The British regularly terrorised the Irish in an attempt to put down even a hint of opposition to their criminal activities. These invading criminals treated the victims as if they were the criminals. If the unfortunates as much as objected to, opposed or even expressed their anti-British feelings, the penalty was often death. More than two hundred "crimes" attracted the death penalty. This was perfectly okay as far as the plunderers were concerned. As they saw it, it was cheaper than jailing the so-called "criminals".

The British inflicted their illegal and cruel activities on the Irish people for more than seven hundred years. They continued to torture and murder right up to the time they moved out of our 26 counties, during the month of December 1922. However, as far as the Catholics in the six counties are concerned, the beat goes on although, I must admit, the situation has improved a lot since then. The British themselves took a number of beatings from the Irish as the centuries elapsed but, by God, our forefathers paid dearly for it. The Irish were active in every county in the country and as the Brits moved their large army of killers into one area to quell an upsurge against their presence, the whole thing would simply erupt in another area.

During the reign of King Henry VIII, County Westmeath was part and parcel of County Meath. Henry concluded that the western side of the county was awash with "criminal activity" and opposition to the presence of the English in Ireland. His answer was to divide the county and, as a result of this, County Westmeath was born. Henry called it a troublesome county but was confident he would sort it out.

As the years passed, the British built three military Barracks in Mullingar to assist the regime dish out rough justice to the people of the town and, indeed, throughout Westmeath. During one week in 1827, 12 men were sentenced to death in Mullingar. They were executed for a variety of "crimes". Locals didn't have to be guilty to be executed – just being Catholic and Irish was sufficient. Suspected membership of the Ribbonmen or the Whiteboys was enough to encourage the authorities to frame a man for a crime they knew he didn't commit.

Policemen from time to time ended up with egg on their faces. One incident springs to mind: it was the crime of the century as far as the people of Mullingar were concerned. In 1827, a number of unknown men actually stole the lead off the courthouse roof, not being satisfied with that, they moved to the Protestant Church at the rear of the courthouse and removed the lead down-pipes. Lead was a valuable commodity. It was used, at that time, to make ball ammunition, slugs, buckshot or whatever. With this in mind the British surely got the lead back in bucketfulls.

This caper took place very close to the town centre and not one person residing in the area heard a thing – or so they told the police. However, in my opinion, every resident except the stone deaf had witnessed the whole shebang. In 1827, there were no nightclubs, discos, ghetto blasters or loud televisions to mask the sound of lead being thrown off the roof, or indeed horse and carts moving in and out of the courtyard as the lads carted the lead away from the scene of the "crime". The "culprits" were never caught, unless they were later apprehended and jailed or executed for an unlinked crime. If this happened in today's world, it would certainly go viral; it would be the laugh of the land. Imagine the Four Courts in Dublin or the Old Bailey in London suffering a similar fate.

On the 24 June 1839, the Marquis of Westmeath, during a speech in the House of Commons, spoke about outrages committed in Mullingar. He went on to say, "during the last fortnight of December 1838 and the first fortnight in January 1839, no less than six murders were committed in County Westmeath alone."

This wasn't the first time the Marquis brought to the attention of Members of Parliament the unruly state of affairs in Westmeath. He spoke about police acting without the assistance of a magistrate and stated that a certain individual was not a fit person to remain in the Commission of Peace.

On the 18 November 1845, Sir Francis Hopkins, Bart (Baronet) and Magistrate, alleged that he was attacked by two "unknown assailants" adding, "I would recognise one of them if I saw him again." The following day, a number of local men were arrested on suspicion. They were brought to Rochfort House, the residence of the alleged victim. Among the suspects was a former tenant, Brian Seery. After Hopkins laid eyes on Seery, he asked to make a second statement. He decided to change his story and accused Seery of being one of the assailants. The *Westmeath Guardian*, a tory newspaper, took immediate action in an attempt to turn decent loyalists against the unfortunate Seery. On the other hand, the same newspaper portrayed Sir Francis Hopkins as a decent gentleman stating, "Sir Francis, no doubt, is to the forefront of the best landlords in Ireland today."

This type of gutter press propaganda was normal practice in Ireland by every loyalist publication down through the years.

On 3 December 1909 The Irish Times published its report on the Joseph Heffernan murder trial. Sadly, this man was executed in January 1910. The editor, staunch loyalist and barrister, John Edward Healy, for reasons best known to himself, altered important witness evidence in what I believe was an attempt to take the heat off the Crown Prosecution team.

Unbelievably, Seery's son, James, was also executed on a trumped-up murder charge. When arrested, James was working as a miner in the Crooked River area of Gippsland, Australia. He was charged with the murder of Auguste Tepfar. Tepfar's headless body and skull were found about 100 yards apart. The decapitated body of his dog was found close by. The police couldn't find a motive to tie Seery to the murder and, according to fellow miners, the two men never fell out.

Tepfar's skull was found in Seery's burning hut and Seery was missing. In my opinion, James was set up. In part two of *I Declare Before My God*, I take the reader through the entire case and give my reasons for believing this young Irishman was innocent of the crime that cost him his life.

The Seery family is just one of the many Irish families that suffered the loss of two members at the hands of the British. To name a few in the Westmeath area, we had the execution of the Kennedy brothers and the Curley brothers in 1827; another set of Curley brothers was executed in 1849 (this was the last public hanging to take place in Mullingar), all at the hands of the British. This type of behaviour was par for the course throughout the 32 counties of Ireland. However, having said that, I must admit that our pro-Treaty Government (yes, the crowd that took over the running of our country from the British) were no better; they also murdered at the drop of a hat. This was our Irish Government and they killed fellow Irishmen in our name, without our blessing.

The anti-Treaty side retaliated with similar atrocities however, before the official commencement of the civil war, the pro-Treaty side together with the British opened fire on unarmed anti-Treaty prisoners being marched down an Irish street. The prisoners had their hands in the air. One was killed and a number injured. Some of the shooters were wearing British army tin hats (helmets).

While the Free State troops were there, the British, in my opinion were involved in most of the shooting. I say this because they wanted to set Irish against Irish and the shooters fired at everyone, including the pro-Treaty soldiers escorting the prisoners. At least one of the pro-Treaty shooters fired high and to this day the bullet holes remain in the wall of a public house. This man was an excellent shot: his grouping displays all the hallmarks of a marksman. My reason for saying he was Irish is because he deliberately fired high for a reason: he didn't want to be responsible for the deaths of fellow Irishmen.

Incidentally, none of this is recorded in the history books. In April 1922 the town in question was described by a number of newspapers as "looking like a battle zone during the Great War." I wrote about it myself in my book, *Why Did They Lie? The Civil War, The Truth, Where and When It Began*, published by The Manuscript Publisher in 2018.

Introduction

The Seery saga began around midnight on 18 November 1845, when Sir Francis Hopkins, Bart (Baronet), alleged that he was shot at and assaulted as he was about to enter his home. Brian Seery was tried and convicted of the alleged crime in January 1846; he was executed on Friday, 13 February the same year. He was found guilty after a second trial – a verdict delivered by a jury packed with members of the aristocracy, ascendancy, gentry, loyalists, magistrates etc. No matter what title I put on these people, it means the same thing – "cold-blooded killers."

In his first statement, Sir Francis Hopkins deposed that he was attacked by two unknown assailants, one of which he said he would recognise if he saw him again. He read and signed this statement so, he was perfectly happy with its content. Two witnesses, local magistrates, Mr Lyons and Mr Reilly also certified the statement as being a true and accurate recording of Hopkins evidence.

However, after the arrest of Seery, a man he knew very well, Hopkins asked to make a second statement in which he said he recognised one of his attackers as Seery. Why would he say this? Of course, he had a reason: money. His love for money took precedence over an innocent Irishman's life. As far as Hopkins was concerned, Seery was nothing more than an Irish Catholic who would later cost him money: a man he needed to get rid of. This "bloodthirsty, country gentleman" lied and in doing so he, together with his fellow "sinister country gentlemen", orchestrated the murder of an innocent man. However, unknown to himself at that time, his actions would also destroy his own life. He later cracked up; he couldn't handle or come to terms with the outcome of his evil deed. I don't believe Hopkins realised Seery would be executed: he assumed the man would be flogged and transported to some faraway land.

Unlike the packed jury and the crooked Crown Prosecutor, I studied the evidence that they felt was strong enough to convict and execute Seery. I believe I have blown the Crown case out of the water.

Seery left behind a young wife, Mary and five young children. Mary, in order to support her family ran a small shop in Seery Street, now Mount Street Mullingar. The locals appropriately renamed the street in honour of her late husband. Mary survived her husband by sixty years. She died a widow on 30 October 1906.

Tragedy afflicting the Seery family didn't end with Brian's death. His son, James, also suffered at the hands of the British. This young man arrived in Australia on board the ship, Lightening, in 1861. He emigrated to seek his fortune but, things didn't work out that way. On arrival, he took up employment on a station (farm), he was happy as he worked on the farm but, the reason he travelled to Australia was to work on the goldfields. A farm labourer's wage was very low. He had very little disposable income at the end of the week. He spent all his spare time searching for employment at the mines and hoping to strike it lucky someday.

James eventually located employment in the mining industry. He took to his new profession like a duck to water. His employers and fellow miners deemed him to be an excellent and honest miner. Nearly ten years after his arrival, James, just like his dad, fell foul of the British regime. He received a custodial sentence for assault, I was unable to locate the file/newspaper reports relating to this incident so, needless to say, I don't know if he was guilty as charged.

The discovery of a skull in the mining village of Crooked River brought James Seery's hopes and aspirations tumbling down. The skull was discovered on 16 September 1870 in the smouldering ashes of Seery's hut. Later, the headless body of a miner was found buried close to the same building. James was arrested, charged, convicted and executed for the murder of his friend, Auguste Tepfar, a miner of German extraction. The police came to the conclusion that the murder took place in the area where the body and head were found, so they focussed all their attention on the village of Crooked River, Gippsland, Australia.

This young man was convicted purely on circumstantial evidence, despite the fact that the evidence didn't make sense. Of course, the British didn't care about James, who, just like his dad, was Irish and Catholic. As far as the British were concerned, when they got their talons stuck into an Irishman, they felt they were entitled to "Hang him High".

Contents

Part I

~ Brian Seery ~

Mullingar, Ireland. 1845-1846

Chapter 1

"Attempted Murder" of Sir Francis Hopkins

The *Westmeath Guardian*, a local Tory newspaper, published an article concerning the alleged attempt on the life of Sir Francis Hopkins. The story appeared two days after the alleged attack. This was adequate time for the authorities and Hopkins to alter their version of events in order to suit and save the baronet's character and indeed, some of his money. The newspaper portrayed this evil man as a saint and some sort of superhuman being.

The writer called the alleged attack, "the most daring and reckless outrage attempted in this county for some years past." He continued, "an attack, which has caused the utmost consternation throughout the neighbourhood, was perpetrated on Tuesday night last on the person of Sir Francis Hopkins, Bart, of Rochfort by two assassins, who lay in wait to take his life but providentially failed in their accursed purpose."

On the night of the alleged attack, Hopkins attended a party at Col Caulfield's home, which is situated on the shores of Lough Ennell and about four miles from Mullingar. He returned home to Rochfort at about half past twelve in the morning. Hopkins let himself out of the carriage. He climbed the steps to the hall door and just as he was about to pull the bell, he alleged that two attackers, who were hiding in the vicinity and awaiting his return from his night out, immediately ran to the steps leading up to the door. He said the two men were armed: one man brandished a long gun and the other man carried a pistol. The man with the gun fired a shot that left eighteen bullets and slugs of all sizes in the door close to where Hopkins was standing.

The writer adds,

> *Hopkins immediately attacked the man with the gun, he got hold of him and a struggle ensued. He was positive he would have apprehended him but for the fact that the second assailant, the man carrying the pistol, on noticing his friend struggling, returned and walked right up to Hopkins. He was so close that he could put his pistol at the breast of Hopkins. He then squeezed the trigger. But for a fortunate stroke of luck, Hopkins would definitely be a dead man. The pistol misfired and merely burned priming.*

The writer continued,

> *Hopkins immediately let go of the first man and attacked the second assailant with such aggression that both fell to the ground. He was over-powered by the two assassins and, as he was unarmed, he called for assistance. There was nobody within earshot; it seems the horses were frightened and out of control after the gun was discharged. The coachman had great difficulty as he endeavoured to extract himself from the box, leaving him unable to assist his master at this crucial time. The would-be assassins launched a vicious attack on Hopkins. They used the pistol and gun as cudgels and inflicted severe injuries to his head. It didn't end there, as the unfortunate Hopkins also received a wound on the cheek: this was caused by the discharge from the gun.*

The writer goes on to say,

> *The assassins were worried that the coachman might sound the alarm and summon assistance from members of the household staff. At this stage, Hopkins had broken free and the assassins ran for the cover of the wood and made their escape. They left behind a hat, coat and pipe. Medical assistance was in attendance with all possible speed and Hopkins wounds attended to promptly. Dr Ferguson gave an update on the victim's condition. He stated, "Hopkins is yet in considerable danger. It is to be hoped that his useful life will be preserved to the country."*

The police were quickly at the scene and immediately began investigating the circumstances surrounding the alleged attack. The writer stated,

> *Hopkins recognised the man who fired the shot and furnished the police with the name and description of this person. Mr Bookey, Sub Inspector, lost no time in apprehending him; he was assisted by Constable Johnston of Dysart station, in whose neighbourhood the attacker was at work. On being brought to Rochfort last night, he was fully identified by Sir Francis Hopkins as the person who fired the bullet and, we also understand that the hat which the assassins left after them has been identified as belonging to the man the police apprehended.*

The writer continues his assessment on Hopkins:

> *It may not be an understatement to say, that he, no doubt, is to the forefront of the best landlords in Ireland today. Since his arrival at Rochfort, he has created employment for about 300 workers (250 seasonal and 50 permanent) and, needless to say, at enormous expense*

– probably running into several thousand pounds. He has been a steward to his tenants; he devoted most of his lifetime to them, running their farming business and this entailed everything and anything in connection with the operation of the farming industry. He taught them the best mode of culture. He assisted them to stock their farms by advancing money to purchase whatever they required to run a successful farm. The financial assistance in question was from £20 to £60 to any of his tenants who required it. He has done an awful lot more than any other landlord that we know of.

When the potato distemper arrived in Westmeath, he took immediate action: he paid to have hundreds of posters and leaflets printed and put them up all over the locality. The posters contained instructions advising the locals on how best to preserve their potato crop and how to make some profit out of the affected potatoes. Whenever he had the opportunity to assist his neighbours and tenants, he wasted no time in doing so. How could the assassins attempt to take the life of such a man and they would have succeeded but for the intervention of Almighty God.

To people who look for reasons to justify such outrageous acts, we will state the facts as they occurred between Sir Francis and Seery. A number of years ago, Seery farmed about 30 acres under Sir F. Hopkins. He was in arrears of rent. Hopkins went to the farm and found it half waste, unstocked and neglected. He approached Seery and explained the reason he was unable to pay rent was due to the fact that he was unable to properly manage a farm of its size.

Seery stated he hadn't the necessary finances to manage the farm in a productive manner. Sir Francis advised him that he would be better off with a smaller farm and offered to buy his interest in the farm he then held. Seery agreed and asked 30 guineas with an acquittance of arrears. Sir Francis agreed to this. They didn't fall out; they never had words. Sir Francis didn't give him notice to quit, nor did he eject him from the farm. Seery agreed to all this.

He asked Sir Francis to recommend him for some small farms that were vacant in the neighbourhood. Sir Francis agreed. Seery looked at some of these farms but felt his life was in danger and was told to prepare his coffin if he took over any of the farms. Lately, Seery has been complaining that his money had run out and regretting the fact that he sold his farm to Sir Francis.

The writer continues:

We should note that Sir Francis could have evicted him for non-title and sued him for failing to pay rent. Sir Francis never turned out a tenant since he came to Westmeath without giving full compensation. He divided

Seery's farm amongst the most deserving of the tenants on the same townland. (*Westmeath Guardian*, Thursday 20 November 1845)

~

My observations:

My response to Hopkins dividing Seery's farm among other tenants is proof that he wanted to increase the rent. However, he couldn't do so as Seery, like most tenants had a lease on the farm. Hopkins bought the lease off Seery for £30 and then he, by getting rid of Seery, reneged on the remainder of the agreement which was to pay the first years rent on Seery's new farm. If what was quoted in the newspaper was true, I believe he would have left Seery with a smaller portion of the farm. This behaviour was common among the landlords at that time.

After learning of the alleged attack on Sir Francis Hopkins, magistrates, members of the gentry and close friends from around Co. Westmeath immediately called to Rochfort House to visit him. Among the magistrates who visited the victim at his residence were the following: Sir Richard Levinge, Baronet; James Gibbon, G. Levinge, J. C. Lyons, W. A. Reilly and R. H. Kelly, Esqs; Col Caulfield; R. Smyth, F. Smith, Thomas. F. Uniacke, W. Featherston, Esqrs; Capt Vignoles; John H. Shiel, R. Swift, T. Lestrange, A. French, Esqrs; Messrs Walsh, County Inspector of Police and Mr Bookey, Sub-Inspector of Police.

Many of his friends who called to see Hopkins were members of the Grand Jury Panel and local magistrates, this says a lot for British justice. While at Rochfort House, these gentlemen decided to submit a requisition to Lord Westmeath, requesting him to convene a meeting of the Magistrates of the county to discuss the attack on Sir Francis Hopkins. They felt it was time to put an end to the outrages that have been perpetrated in the county since the last assizes. The meeting was arranged for the following Tuesday.

Chapter 2

Special Commission – Assizes

On account of the increased criminal activity in the area, the authorities decided to set up a Special Commission, or Assizes, in Mullingar. In reality, the intention of the British was to deal quickly and harshly with Brian Seery, as they wanted to make an example out of this man. This type of treatment, they believed, would let the locals know, in no uncertain terms, that they will not tolerate an attack on any member of the gentry. As usual, the British never let the fact that a defendant was innocent get in the way.

~

Westmeath Guardian **Report 22 January 1846**

Mr Murphy Q.C., Mr Gorman, Mr Gunning and Mr J.A. Curran counsel were assigned by the crown to represent all defendants awaiting trial that week. These men arrived some days before the assizes commenced and they spent the time available preparing a defence for the prisoners. Mr H.G. Curran and Mr Rooney were also in attendance. The day before the commencement of the assizes, the Lord Chief Justice of the Common Pleas and the Lord Chief Baron of the Exchequer arrived in town. The following morning, the judges entered the court at 11am, at which time the proceedings began.

Chief Justice Doherty addressed the Grand Jury as follows:

> *Gentlemen of the Grand jury, the state of this county has been such for the last five months that it became necessary for you to assemble at this unusual period and within a few weeks of your been empanelled at your ordinary Assizes. However, on looking at the official return of outrages which have been inflicted on the people since the last Assizes and on considering their character and number, I am not surprised that those who naturally feel the deepest interest in the welfare of this county should endeavour to speedily put an end to this state of affairs and by a prompt administration of the law, to overrule the disturbers of the public peace, to afford security and protection to the unoffending and industrious and to restore tranquillity and order.*

Gentlemen, I do not intend to enlarge on the disastrous consequences which would result from allowing your county to suffer any longer in the state in which, unhappily, it has been in for some months past. I purposely and studiously abstain from doing so because I am anxious to avoid averting to any topic calculated to inflame or to disturb the calmness with which it is desirable that all who take part in the administration of the criminal law should approach the discharge of their solemn and important duties.

Gentlemen, from the experience I have so frequently had of the manner in which you discharge your duties as Grand Jurors, I feel that you do not require any explanation or instruction from the court. I have the fullest reliance on the vigilance and attention with which you will proceed in the examination of the different charges that will be brought before you. You will, I have no doubt, act firmly and temperately and will not, I am satisfied, suffer any indignation at the outrages which have been committed to excite a prejudice in your minds when you are weighing the evidence against each individual accused. However, those who have been engaged in the outrages which we deplore have insulted and violated the laws. I hope we shall let them see that those laws will be administered on the present occasion, not more for the punishment of the guilty than the protection of the innocent or even of those with respect to whose guilt there can exist a reasonable doubt. With these few observations I shall dismiss you for the consideration of the business that has been prepared for your information.

~

This pre-trial address by the judge was par for the course and always loaded against the unfortunate defendant. This, together with a packed jury, invariably secured a guilty verdict. On top of that, prior to the start of a trial, the Crown Prosecutor would unofficially sit down with members of the Grand Jury and point out to them the importance of delivering a guilty verdict. However, he knew full well he would achieve his desired outcome, as members of the gentry, staunch loyalists and even magistrates sat on juries appointed to hear criminal cases, and Seery's case was no different. The Grand Jury returned to their room and Bills of Indictment were immediately placed before them. Half an hour later, a true Bill was returned against Brian Seery.

~

Westmeath Guardian continued:

> *The defendant was placed at the bar and the indictment containing twelve counts was read to him, he pleaded not guilty to all the charges. He was advised of his right to challenge twenty persons without cause and as many more as he could show cause for.*
>
> *Mr Murphy Q.C., assisted by Messrs Curran and Gorman, said that on hearing the indictment read, he perceived that some of the counts were for a capital offence and some for a misdemeanour, and he thought the best stage of the case was to require the Crown to make their selection of which they intended to proceed on.*
>
> *The Attorney General said that it was not a case in which the Crown was called on to make a selection.*
>
> *The Judges agreed in opinion with the Prosecution.*
>
> *The Jury Panel was then called over, filling the galleries and boxes to capacity. After the calling of the panel had been proceeded with for some time, the Attorney General rose and announced that as eighty-four jurors having answered, it was his opinion that it would be a more waste of time to proceed further with the list, unless counsel for the Defence required it.*
>
> *Mr Murphy, having declared that he was satisfied with the number in attendance, the following jury was empanelled: William M. Maxton, Esq; William Dawson, Esq; John H. Shiel, Esq; J.P. Richard Swift, Esq; J.P. Edward Lewis, Esq; Bernard Delany, Esq; L.L. Henry, Esq; J.P. Anthony Matthews, Esq; George Daly, Esq; Gerald Fitzgerald, Esq; John Hodson, Esq; J.P. and Hugh W. Shell, Esq.*
>
> *The defendant was then formally arraigned and given in charge for firing at Sir Francis Hopkins. The Attorney General applied to have the witnesses removed from the court. The Chief Baron gave direction accordingly and said that any witnesses remaining would run the risk of a severe fine.*

Chapter 3

Brian Seery's Trial – 20 January 1846

Westmeath Guardian **Report 22 January 1846**

The Attorney General, in opening the case for the Crown, said that, from the abstract of the indictment that they the jury had heard read, they would no doubt understand the general nature of the offences with which the defendant, Brian Seery, is charged.

> *It was one of numerous cases that sadly occurred in the Mullingar area over a short period of time and which disgraced the entire county. From the nature and number of these offences, it was vitally important to call the county together on this very extraordinary occasion, with the belief that by a prompt and effective administration of the law, the progress of such crime may be arrested.*

It was thought necessary to issue a Special Commission in order to investigate the serious attack on Sir Francis Hopkins. This was a case in which the evidence appeared to him (the Attorney General) to be of so clear and satisfactory a nature, as to warrant an expectation that the perpetrators of the offence would be brought to a speedy justice. This case was of that category. The Crown did not call on the jury for a guilty verdict unless it appeared to them that the evidence was of that nature to render it clear. If the evidence was as satisfactory as he believed, he was quite confident that the jury would discharge with firmness and integrity the all-important duty they had to perform.

> *The defendant is charged with attempting to take the life of Sir Francis Hopkins, Bart, of Rochfort, Mullingar, a magistrate of the county. The prisoner is charged with having committed that crime and a number of other crimes in the company of person's unknown.*

He would shortly inform them of the exact state of the law now before them.

Morally speaking, an attempt to take away the life of a person was an offence, fully and of as deep a dye as that of actual murder: as the intention of the assailant who committed the crime amounted to murder. Formally, an attempt to commit the crime was a capital offence even though, the attempt should fail and, no bodily injury should result.

Of late, it was decided by the legislature to modify the law in this respect. The change in the regulation of the criminal law, to some extent, mitigated the punishment of attempted murder. Now, it is not a capital offence to make an attempt to take away life, provided no bodily harm was sustained in the attempt to commit the murder. He read the new regulations and said they are well known and also, the clause in the Act of Parliament on this issue.

He also read the clause under which the prisoner was indicted. The defendant was charged, in the first instance, with being one of two persons who fired at and assaulted Sir Francis Hopkins, with intent to commit murder. The prisoner was also charged with having discharged a loaded gun at Sir Francis Hopkins, with intent to commit murder. The prisoner was also charged with having discharged a loaded pistol at Sir Francis Hopkins, with like intent and also, with having cut and wounded him with intent to maim and disfigure him. He also stated the facts to the jury and would say that he would support the facts with evidence, such as would leave no doubt that the several charges, or each, or some of them would be sustained.

The Prosecution's Case

Sir Francis Hopkins is a sitting magistrate of the county and resides at Rochfort House, Mullingar. The attack occurred on 18 November last. Sir Francis dined at the house of Colonel Caulfield, who resided about a mile and a half from Rochfort. A number of years ago, the prisoner was a tenant to Sir Francis Hopkins, from whom he held a farm but had not the means to carry it on, as he could not stock or cultivate it. He therefore surrendered the land in the year 1842 and Sir Francis gave him £30 for doing so. Everything was arranged up to that time in a satisfactory manner between them.

The Attorney General added:

> *I mentioned this, not for the purpose of explaining what might have been the motive of the prisoner in committing the crime of which he is accused but, for the purpose of showing that he was known to Sir Francis Hopkins, who had many opportunities of seeing and knowing him and he was well acquainted with his person and face.*

On the 18 November last, Sir Francis returned from Colonel Caulfield's and when he got out of his carriage at the hall door of his house, an assailant fired a shot at him with a gun. This was definitely an attempt to murder him: its contents, bullets and slugs were lodged in the hall door close to where

Sir Francis was standing. There is no doubt that the gun was charged with deadly material.

Sir Francis appeared to be a man possessing great courage: he immediately pursued the assailant and seized him. During the struggle between them for the gun, a second person appeared and snapped a pistol at Sir Francis, clearly with the intent of shooting him, which the first man failed to accomplish. The pistol misfired and a struggle took place between Sir Francis and the second man. Sir Francis was knocked down and the attackers then ran away, as an alarm had been given.

During the struggle with the first person, Sir Francis had recognised and could identify the defendant and there could be no doubt about it. Seery was not seen for the first time by Sir Francis that night, as they were well acquainted with each other.

Several blows were inflicted on Sir Francis by the second attacker and then, the assailants made their escape after laying his skull bare. He received other severe injuries that kept him laid up for a long time, under medical treatment. He had narrowly escaped with his life.

Shortly after the occurrence, Sir Francis gave an account of the attack and this resulted in the arrest of Seery. A coat and hat were found on the grounds, near the place where the outrage was committed and, the Prosecution would prove that these articles belonged to Seery.

The case for the Crown was short and simple and the Attorney General could not anticipate what case could be made for the prisoner, as he believed Seery's guilt was so very clear. He believed the jury would give the evidence their fullest attention and, unless the case for the Crown was much shaken with regard to truth, the jury would, of course, find a verdict of guilty. However, if they had any reasonable doubt as to the guilt of the prisoner, they would give it to him and find a verdict of not guilty.

The Evidence for the Prosecution

Sir Francis Hopkins, examined by Mr Sergeant Warren, said that he resides at Rochfort House in this county, about four miles from Mullingar, he is a magistrate. He went to dinner at 7 o'clock in a small carriage driven by his servant (an Englishman), who had been about two months here at the time. He went to dine at Col Caulfield's and left it at about 25 minutes past 12. There was a large party, about twenty persons, in attendance. He was perfectly sober on leaving Col Caulfield's. There was no moon but, it was a dusky, twilight night.

He let himself down from the carriage; the servant remained on the box seat. He had just walked up the steps and pulled the bell when he heard the shot and saw the smoke. A man was standing where the smoke was. The man ran away and he followed him about 35 yards, to a steep bank, when he (Hopkins) fell and the attacker fell too. He caught hold of the man with the gun in his hand and he wrestled with him, in an attempt to take the gun from him. When he failed to take the gun off him, he caught the attacker by the neck and throttled him.

He recognised the assailant the very moment he saw him. He was so amazed at who it was and to be positive of his identity, he forced his attacker's head up to take his profile and satisfy himself that Seery was the person.

He looked behind and he saw a man coming towards him. The man was about ten yards away at the time. He let Seery go and advanced towards the man. When within two feet of the witness, this man pulled the trigger of a cavalry pistol but, it misfired. The witness swung a severe blow with his left hand and knocked the oncoming attacker down.

He looked around and saw the first man come with the gun. He had the muzzle in his hand and intended to strike the witness. The witness grabbed the man. A struggle ensued when the attacker, who had the pistol, came and struck him, bringing him down on one knee. He repeated his blows a number of times. Sir Francis cried for help, someone opened the hall door and, with light shining from the premises, the assailants, in order to hide their identity, ran off as fast as they could.

Hopkins said he saw Seery the following day and added:

I see him now standing in the dock. I have no doubt that he was the person who fired the shot. I know him for about eight years. I was his landlord and he surrendered a farm to me in 1842. I paid him £30 as remuneration. I served him with neither notice to quit nor an ejectment order. On going over his farm one day, I found it not even half stocked or fully cropped. I confronted him and asked how much money he would take for his interest. He asked me for £30. I agreed and gave him the money. I also agreed to assist him as he looked for a new farm and I promised to pay the first year's rent. Seery appeared very happy with the agreement; I never heard that he had a problem with it. I gave him a written recommendation when he was searching for another farm.
When I seized him, he had no hat on. The hat which I had seen him wear for a considerable period was a peculiar one. I saw a hat the following morning; it's the same which I had seen Seery often wear. A coat was also found; it is the same as he came, more than once, to Rochfort in. I had five or six wounds and they were very severe, I was a month under medical care. Dr Ferguson was with me in the course

of an hour after the occurrence, I gave a description and named the person who had fired at me. The prisoner is that person.

A short cut and peculiarly shaped hat was exhibited to Sir Francis Hopkins, which he said was like the hat that Seery was in the habit of wearing.

Cross examined by Mr Murphy Q.C., Sir Francis said,

I did not find the hat myself.

A paper was handed to Sir Francis, which he said was in his handwriting. It was the recommendation alluded to by Sergeant Warren.

I may have told this transaction fifty times but, I think not one hundred times. I have told it both before and after dinner. I told it to a great many gentlemen of the county. I did not detail it to any of the jury. The only person on the jury that I could have possibly told it to is Mr Sheil, as I think he was one of the Magistrates who attended the investigation but, I am not sure. I saw the hat on the following morning and I identified it.

Mr Murphy handed in the first information sworn by Sir Francis and said there was no mention made either of Seery or the hat. The second information was also handed to him and read, and the hat was not mentioned. Sir Francis said,

I made two informations: one before and the other after Seery was arrested. I saw Seery the following evening at Rochfort. It was about five o'clock. I saw him in the hall of Rochfort. Several magistrates and country people were present. I know not who the country people were but Seery was among them. Seery's name does not appear in the first information but, it does in the second. There is nothing about the coat in either of them. The hat was given to me by Thomas Telling, my butler, the next morning. I know not if he be in town. Constable Johnston was the first who showed me the coat, at five o'clock the following day. I don't know if Johnston has sworn informations or not. I never spoke to Johnston or any other constable about the hat. I did not speak to Johnston about the coat. He may have heard me talk about it while I was telling other people I could identify it. The prisoner ceased to be my tenant in September 1842. He called on me several times after that. He called to my residence during September and October last. We parted as good friends in 1842. I had no reason to complain of Seery's character and conduct while he was a tenant. If he had capital to manage his farm, I would have been happy to continue him as a tenant. I find it difficult to believe that he would attempt to take my life. I really believed he would protect me if I required it.

Re-examined by Sergeant Warren, Sir Francis said:

Seery came over one morning and asked me for a character reference. I should have mentioned that I agreed to put him in possession of a farm and pay a year's rent for him but, seemingly, on going to look at the farm, he was intimidated by threats and declined it. When he chose to act for himself and forfeit that for which I was engaged, I gave him a general recommendation according to what he had ability for and what he was competent to manage but, I could not recommend him for a large farm.

William Pallinger, examined by Mr Brewster, said that on the 18 November last, he was in the service of Sir Francis Hopkins and drove him to and from Col Caulfield's that night. On arrival back to Rochfort, his master opened the carriage door himself and walked up the steps. There was no noise. The witness observed two men running towards him while he was turning the carriage. One man tripped and fell down; the other came on and fired a shot. He was, at the time, 6 or 7 yards from Sir Francis and within a yard of the first step. The assassin was at the side of the steps. He (witness) had not quite turned the carriage when the shot was fired. The men ran away and, his master followed. The mare plunged. Witness got down as quick as he could and pulled the bell and then ran to his master's assistance. The men were out of sight when witness reached his master. He found him just getting up and assisted him. (Pallinger was not cross-examined).

Matthew Rogers, Steward to Sir Francis Hopkins, was examined. He said that he remembers the night Sir Francis Hopkins was attacked. He said, he found a coat and tobacco pipe the following morning. He brought the coat into the hall and saw it after in the charge of Mr Bookey. He said he was shown a hat that morning by Thomas Telling.

The hat now produced is the hat as shown to me. The great coat now produced is the same which I found that morning. I found the coat about 40 yards from the house at seven o'clock on the morning, after my master was attacked.

To the Chief Justice:

I found the coat lying outside the railings on the ground.

To the jury:

> *It appeared to me that the coat had been taken off and laid down with the collar uppermost. It had not the appearance of been taken off in a struggle.*

Thomas Telling, sworn and examined, stated that on 18 November last, he was in the employment of Sir Francis Hopkins. He said he found a hat close to where Sir Francis was. He gave the hat to Mr Rogers, steward at Rochfort. Sir Francis was standing at the time he reached him and, the assailants were gone. He found the hat and his master a little after the shot was fired. It was about 12 o'clock at night. It might have been a quarter of an hour before or after it.

Constable Johnston, who was examined by Mr Plunkett, said he belongs to the Constabulary and is stationed at Dysart. He knows the prisoner for about six years. He had frequent opportunities of seeing him and did see him. He generally wore nice clothes and cord breeches. In his working habit, he wore a low, short-cut hat with the crown stitched in. The hat now produced is the one he used to wear.

Cross-examined by Mr Gorman, he said he knew Seery for about six years and cannot tell, at present, any other man in the county whose hat he would swear to. He saw the prisoner three weeks before the shooting at Sir Francis Hopkins. He did not then wear the hat. He cannot say when, before the three weeks, he had seen him. He saw him about a month before then and he wore a "jerry hat" –

> *... a hard-felt hat is what I mean by a jerry hat. He did not wear the hat now produced on that occasion. I cannot say exactly when before that period I saw him but, I think it was about two months. I will not say what hat he wore then. I saw him frequently in the middle of summer wear that hat at Rathnamuddagh, where I am stationed. I never had the hat in my hand 'til it was given to me for identification, after the attack on Sir Francis Hopkins. The county inspector (Mr Walsh) and his servant were present when I saw the hat. A person named Doherty was not present then. I did not arrest the prisoner. I cannot say that the present band was on it in summer last, or what band was on it then. I cannot be mistaken in the hat; it is the same that I frequently saw him wear.*

Constable Doherty, sworn and examined by the Attorney General, stated,

> *I am stationed at Dysart and have been there two years and some months. I know the prisoner and frequently saw him. The hat now produced, I often saw him wear. I have no doubt but that it is the very same hat that I saw on the prisoner.*

Cross-examined by Mr Curran, Doherty said that the prisoner lived near Dysart for about six months,

> ... *he lived at Rathdrishogue. I heard he lived there but cannot say how long. I would swear to other hats as well as the present one. I saw him wear that hat in summer last but, I don't know the month. I saw him pass the barracks last summer but never spoke to him. I never had the hat in my hand 'til after the attack on Sir Francis Hopkins.*

To the jury, Doherty stated:

> *There are no hats of that appearance near the station or anywhere else in the neighbourhood.*

Dr Ferguson, sworn and examined by Mr Sergeant Warren, stated:

> *I am a surgeon; I recollect the night of the 18 November last. I arrived at Rochfort shortly before two o'clock the morning of the 19th. I found Sir Francis labouring under severe wounds. There were two on the left side of the forehead. In one of them, the bone was laid perfectly bare for two inches. Over the left ear, there was a very ugly contused wound one-and-a-half inches. There were two of the smaller kind over it and two others under. In that point, there were five beside the two wounds on the forehead. there was a smaller circular wound on the cheek but not of much consequence. The first two were inflicted by a heavy blunt instrument. The wound over the ear had the appearance of being inflicted by the cock of the pistol. He never had a case of wounds in the head which threatened greater danger. He was in extreme danger. I saw marks on the hall door of 2 bullets and 14 or 15 slugs. Sir Francis Hopkins told me that night, that he knew the person that attacked him and that he was a tenant of his, and I communicated it to Mr Bookey, in consequence of which, the prisoner was arrested.*

Cross-examined by Mr Murphy, he said, "I was in the house next day but not at the investigation. I was not there when Seery was produced," he added. "I swore to the wounds that Sir Francis had received on 24 November."

Re-examined by Mr Warren, he stated:

> *As well as I recollect, the prisoner Seery was arrested before I swore my informations.*

The case for the Crown closed here and Mr Murphy, on behalf of the prisoner, asked permission to postpone his address until he concluded the examination of the witnesses for the Defence and, gave from a precedent

"Crawford and Dix", which occurred on this circuit. It appears that the Crown consented.

The Crown opposed the present application and the privilege was not granted.

The prisoner's counsel asked permission to retire for a few minutes to confer on the course that they should take.

The Chief Justice:

Certainly, as long as you require, Mr Murphy.

Chapter 4

Brian Seery's Defence

Westmeath Guardian Report 22 January 1846

Mr Murphy opened the case for the Defence by stating that it became his duty to address the jury for the prisoner, who was on trial for his life. He said that the time was unexpected and had the trial taken place at the ordinary time, when no prejudice or excitement prevailed on the subject, he would rely on a verdict at once for the prisoner. The law respected no man and jurors should do the same.

If a humble peasant came on the table (Bench) that day and gave such an account of that transaction as Sir Francis Hopkins did, would not the jury, on the instant, acquit the prisoner? He said he did not impeach Sir Francis Hopkins because of the transaction: he believes that he had acted gallantly and defended himself. But he (Mr Murphy) would show that Sir Francis Hopkins had made a mistake, which was, indeed, very natural under the circumstances as he was then placed in. Great crimes are not committed without some motive and what motive could induce the prisoner to the commission of the crime imputed to him.

Mr Murphy went on to say that he would read a letter written by Sir Francis Hopkins – a letter that gives a character to the prisoner in the highest terms. The Attorney General, in opening the case, said that there was an expression of ill feeling used by the prisoner but, Sir Francis had stated that no such thing had taken place. Sir Francis was the prisoner's benefactor and had given him a good character reference. Was this the man to imbrue his hands in the blood of that man? Men do not become assassins all at once and, instead of going to shoot Sir Francis Hopkins, the prisoner had the strongest inducements to preserve and not destroy the life of the man who was to be his benefactor and protector – for, Sir Francis had promised even to pay a year's rent for the prisoner.

The whole case rested on the evidence of identification, as given by Sir Francis Hopkins, who had an opportunity of seeing the person only in the dead and dark hour of the night, after coming from a party. Sir Francis swore an information the next day but, the name of the prisoner was not mentioned. He read the information before signing. Would they credit a humble servant who would swear such an information? Was it not natural that the first thing a man would say was to tell the name of the party who fired at him?

The only thing that he swore in his first information, was that he would know one of the men again. If he were satisfied of Seery being one of the attackers, why not say so at once, or even the next day, when the magistrates were assembled. Did he state the name of the party before whom he swore the information? No, and if he had, the Crown would have produced them to sustain the case, instead of the medical witness who was brought in to prop up the case. He did not throw any disrepute on the surgeon. The prisoner was a tenant of Sir Francis Hopkins and, did the latter state that Seery was the man who fired at him after he was arrested on suspicion and brought before Sir Francis Hopkins? That was the first time that the name of Seery was mentioned and, had his name been mentioned to the magistrates before? If so, would not the magistrates be present to corroborate the statement?

Sir Francis Hopkins had made a mistake and he (Mr Murphy) was in a position to prove it. With reference to the evidence given by the police, it was truly painful to witness the exhibition they had made there that day. If human lives were to depend on the evidence as given by them, no man in society could be safe.

They never had the hat in their hands and only saw it at a distance but, when and where they could not tell and yet, the jury were called upon to take away the life of the prisoner at the bar, on the proof of the identity of a peasant's hat. God forbid that people's lives should depend on such evidence, or that a jury could be found to convict a man on a capital felony on such evidence. It was six days after the prisoner was arrested that the informations were sworn by the police about the hat, although they knew well of the finding of the hat. He would ask them, as honest and con-acre men, could they find a verdict of guilty against the prisoner? He would now proceed to give proof that would save the prisoner's life, without even a doubt as to his guilt. He would account for the prisoner on that night, by persons of respectability and beyond all doubt. The story that would be told was that the prisoner, after losing his farm, took potato ground from his uncle, a man named Thomas Kiernan, a most respectable farmer. On the Monday before the outrage, the prisoner went to dig his potatoes and was asleep eight miles from Rochfort at the time Sir Francis Hopkins was attacked. Mr Murphy said that he would now prove his case.

Elizabeth Kiernan, an old woman, examined by Mr Gorman, was the wife of Thomas Kiernan. She lived in Rathdrishogue, near Castletown. She heard of Sir Francis Hopkins being fired at when Brian Seery was taken prisoner. Mrs Kiernan said:

Brian was digging potatoes on my husband's land, convenient to my house when he was taken. My husband is uncle to the prisoner. The prisoner came the Monday before, to dig con-acre potatoes that he had from my husband. He slept at my house on Monday night. I left him on that night about ten o'clock with the family. I was up before him in the morning and he was there. He returned to the house on Tuesday, after work. He went out with my son, John Kiernan, to see the cattle, went to bed and left the family at the fire. I was up first in the house that morning and he and John Kiernan very soon came downstairs, the door was not unlocked 'til my son and the prisoner came down. My husband was in the County Meath and returned the day after the prisoner been taken. My son and three daughters were in the house on Tuesday night. They were churning on that night 'til a late hour. Seery was there the whole time the churning was going on. I saw him when he came in on Monday morning and he wore a flax hat. He brought nothing with him save the clothes he was wearing. He never changed his clothes during the time he was here. His great coat was hung in the hall whilst he was at work. The police took it away a day or two after his arrest.

Crossed examined by the Attorney General, she stated:

Brian Seery is nephew to my husband. Monday was the first time he slept at my house since he went to live in Mullingar. He came early on Monday morning. Mullingar is six miles from where I live. The defendant had potatoes with us last season. He then lived at Jamestown, which is more than a mile from us. Last year, he did not sleep at my house whilst digging his potatoes, as his own house was so near. I could not say what time he quit digging. He dug 'til dark. The doors are locked every night. The prisoner and his man, Myles Dalton, Michael Finn (my servant boy) and my own family were all there that Monday night. John Burns remained 'til ten o'clock and then went away. There are three rooms upstairs and a parlour, kitchen and cellar on the ground floor. My husband was away both Monday and Tuesday at Summerhill. He was seeing a brother of his. The police took Seery's coat from my house on Thursday morning. this was two days after the attack on Sir Francis Hopkins. John Kiernan and Brian Seery supped in the parlour. The other men took supper in the kitchen. My three daughters and myself took our supper at the kitchen fire whilst the men were at theirs. On Monday night, both Seery and John Kiernan had cold meat for supper because they did not come home for dinner. I sent

*out for John but, he was looking after the cattle and could not come in.
Bacon and cold goose was what they had. Seery had better than one
half-acre of potatoes planted.*

Re-examined by Mr Murphy, she said:

*The men quit at the usual time for working. Her husband holds 70
acres of land. The persons in the house were: Myles Dalton, Mick
Finn, Brian Seery, John Kiernan, my three daughters and John Burns,
who went home.*

Mary Kiernan, examined by Mr Curran, stated:

*I am daughter of the last witness. My father's name is Thomas
Kiernan. We live at Rathdrishogue. The prisoner is a relative of mine.
He was in our house in November last whilst digging potatoes. I don't
know how much land he had. He came on Monday and was arrested
on Wednesday. He had with him two workmen. He supped that
Monday evening with my brother and slept with my brother. I saw him
before sunrise in the morning after getting up. His potatoes were
planted close to the house. He returned from work on Tuesday evening
accompanied by Myles Dalton and my brother. He supped in the
parlour. I also supped in the parlour but not with them. Michael Finn,
Myles Dalton, John Burns and my brother were in the house. They
were after churning and had butter for supper. My brother and Finn
went out to the stable to see the cattle after supper but, I can't say that
Seery went with them. I saw the prisoner go upstairs to bed. I can't tell
who went to bed last. Myles Dalton and Mick Finn slept in the kitchen;
my father was at Summerhill, seeing his brother, who is the parish
priest there. I saw Seery go to work in the morning and he was taken
by the police about one o'clock. He came to our house with an oiled
hat, cord breeches and bang-up coat.*

Cross-examined by Mr Brewster, Mary Kiernan said:

*I recollect the morning of the day that Seery came to our house. I do
not recollect who took supper on Monday evening. Brian Seery had
potatoes and milk for dinner on Monday. I do not know whether my
brother and Seery dined together. I sat on Monday evening and supped
by myself. I can't say what my sister took for supper. There were
potatoes there for my mother and sisters but, I can't say whether they
ate any or not. I think I remained in the kitchen for a while after my
supper. I then went to the parlour. Both Seery and my brother supped
there but my brother went out to see the cattle after supper and Seery
went to the kitchen. Seery went to see his friends, the Killion's, before*

he returned to the house from digging that evening. He had supper about nine o'clock. He dined about one o'clock on Tuesday and returned about the usual hour of quitting in the evening. I supped by myself in the parlour on Tuesday evening. None of the family was with me. I had potatoes and butter. Seery and my brother supped before me in the parlour and had potatoes, milk and butter. Myles Dalton, John Burns and Mick Finn supped in the kitchen. I saw my sisters sup at the kitchen fire. My brother went to the stable about ten o'clock. I did not see Seery since he went to live in Mullingar before that Monday. He had a few ridges of potatoes the year before from my father. Seery has a wife and five children who, at present, reside at Brewery Yard, Mullingar. Immediately after supper, my brother lit a candle and he and Finn went to the stable but, I cannot say whether the prisoner accompanied him or not.

(A written statement was handed to the witness, which she admitted having signed. It set forth that she gave her brother and Seery their supper and that after supper, they sat at the kitchen fire until bedtime and that Brian Seery did not go out with her brother).

On re-examination by Mr Curran, she stated:

Mr French, the magistrate and a policeman, brought me upstairs and took down my examination. Mr French read it over and I signed it but, I thought I told him that I did not know whether Seery went out or not. I did not read the paper which I signed.

Catherine Kiernan, sister of the last witness, gave similar testimony on her direct examination to that deposed by her sister.

Cross examined by Mr Clarke, she said:

I can't tell how long I know Seery but, I know him since he was a little boy. I was never at his house. I saw a hat with the crown sewn in, like that produced. I saw him go to his room that Tuesday night and shut the door after him. I was standing on the lobby at the time. I always locked the hall door and left the key in it. I went into the parlour whilst they were eating their supper. On Monday, I supped in the kitchen with my mother and sisters. On Tuesday night, my brother, Seery and Mick Finn went to the stable and returned again and went to bed.

She added:

... we churned on Tuesday evening and had it finished about nine o'clock.

To a juror, she said:

> *I locked the hall door on Monday and Tuesday and left the key in it. I think the prisoner could not get out. My mother never locks it unless I am away from home.*

John Kiernan, son of Thomas Kiernan and brother of former witnesses gave similar testimony on his direct examination and further deposed that the prisoner slept with him on the nights of Monday and Tuesday. He stated,

> *On the latter evening, I went to the stable. I was accompanied by Mick Finn and we rubbed two horses. Seery, the prisoner, held the candle for us whilst doing so. I returned with Seery and Finn in about fifteen minutes. We sat at the fire and retired to bed about ten o'clock or half past ten o'clock. Brian Seery slept with me that night and did not quit my room 'til we both got up in the morning. It was not possible for Seery to get up and leave my room and return to it again without my knowledge. I was never at Rochfort House but, I have seen it at a distance; it is eight miles from my father's place. To go to Rochfort, a person should walk around eight miles or row across the lake. I saw Mr French the day after Seery was arrested. It was in the room where Seery and I slept. He took down a statement and read it for me and I signed it. There was no one present but the police. I did not read it at all.*

Cross-examined by Mr Brewster, he stated:

> *I live about a mile and a half from the lake of Dysart, nearly in line with Rochfort House. I never, in all my life, crossed the lake. I was in a boat on the lake that I got at Lilliput, about one-and-a-quarter miles from my house but I never crossed the lake. I know a person named Doyle but never knew he kept a boat for hire, I can't tell whose boat I was in. I was not on the lake for many years. Seery came shortly after sunrise on Monday morning. I was looking that day at the stock. I dined at home that Monday in the kitchen, I came home without being sent for by my mother. Myles Dalton, John McDonnell, Mick Finn, John Burns and Brian Seery and myself dined together. My mother and sisters did not dine with us: it is not their habit to do so when there are men in the house. I supped that evening in the parlour. There was no fire in it. Myself and Seery had potatoes and meat. I had a bit of beef and some goose meat. The beef was bought in Mullingar. It was a stewed goose cooked the day before. I could not tell who dined on Sunday or, whether my mother or sisters dined or, who carved or partook of the goose. I could recollect perfectly what occurred on Monday but could not think how we dined on Sunday. I recollect*

Monday because, Mr French asked me a few days afterwards what took place on Monday and Tuesday.
I do not know if it was the same goose that was stewed on Sunday – a good part of it was gone. I had part of the quarter on Monday night. My sister, Catherine, cut it up and helped us and did not take any of it herself. I was quite sure all this took place on the Monday night; there could be no mistake about it. On Tuesday night, I had supper of potatoes and butter, a plate of meat was also on the table but none of the meat was eaten. We were sent to the parlour by my mother to take our supper. I cannot recollect where I supped the night Mr French called. The first thing I did after supper was to go to the stable and Seery and Finn were with me. I went to bed first and Seery followed me about two minutes later. A statement taken by Mr French and signed by the witness was about being read but, Mr Murphy objected to it being received as evidence, as the witness had not read it before signing. Their Lordships decided that it could not be received as an independent document but, the witness could be questioned with regard to the truth of the statements it contained.

He was accordingly questioned about it but, the discrepancies were not very material. He stated that Brian Seery had an old hat, similar to the one produced in evidence, with an old bottom sewed in the top of it.

Patrick Donohue, sworn and examined stated, he knows the prisoner as he lived at witness's house and left last May. The witness produced an old hat. The mould was stitched and a part of the leaf was sewn. The witness said that it belonged to Brian Seery. Mr Gunning, agent to the prisoner, was at his house enquiring for it. The hat was on a stack of oats, where it was put to frighten the crows. When he heard of the hat found at Sir Francis Hopkins, he took it off the stack and threw it on the loft, where it remained from that time until Thursday last.

Cross-examined by the Attorney General, he stated:

I live in Adamstown, about seven miles from Mullingar. Seery lived at my house up to May last year. The hat was not in much better condition since Seery left. I knew it was his hat but, I never told him I had it. I put it on the stack to keep off the crows. It was in the house from about May 'til Christmas. I don't know how long it was on the stack: no one came to look for it at the time I took it off the stack and put it on the loft. I heard that he lost his old hat and I thought it would be needed for the present trial. I never told Brian Seery a word about it although, I kept it for the trial. I told Mr Gunning that I had the like and I sent it in on Thursday last. I saw Brian twice in the gaol after I took the hat off the stack and I did not tell him one word about it.

To a juror:

> *It was an English felt hat Seery wore when going away. It was not a glazed hat. The hat was not put on the stack 'til after the corn was put into the haggard, sometime in November.*

Myles Dalton, sworn and examined, stated that he lives in Mullingar; he is lodging with the wife of the prisoner; he works every day for any person who hires him. He went for a load of potatoes to Adamstown and the old hat was sent in with him but, he was not sent out to collect it. Pat Donohue sent it in with witness and told him to take it home. He stood at the ladder and saw him hand it down off the loft.

> *I was just going home at the time and Donohue asked me to take it. I saw the prisoner at the gaol in about a fortnight after his committal but, never said a word about the hat. I told Seery's wife, after he being arrested, that it was at Donohue's. I knew the old hat was there from when at work with him. I heard the prisoner say that he should get his hat covered and that he should remain until it would be finished, as he had nothing to wear. I asked where the old one was and, he said it was at Donohue's. At the time the short commission was spoken of, I went to Donohue's about a week or ten days after the prisoner being taken. I went there to dig some potatoes and I heard the children saying that Seery's hat was there. Some of the children are 20 years of age. I did not ask to see it, nor did I see it, nor do I know where it was. I slept on the loft that night and had light going to bed but, I did not look for the hat. I was arrested and brought before Sir Francis for shooting at him. I was last up at Kiernan's that night. The servant boy and I slept in the kitchen and I did not go out 'til morning.*

Re-examined, Witness stated:

> *A glazed cover was merely sewn and drawn on the hat, the doing of which did not take many minutes.*

To the jury:

> *I brought the hat to Seery's wife, on my return to town.*

The Rev Andrew Mangan, P.P. Dysart (some reports named the priest as the Rev Maguire, P.P. Dysart) examined, stated that he knows the prisoner for the last twenty years and never heard anything to his disadvantage before the present. He never knew him to be summoned or brought before a magistrate for any offence.

Mr Sergeant Warren replied to evidence and the statement made by counsel in opening the Defence. In a clear and eloquent manner, he pointed out the discrepancies of the witness's brought up to prove the alibi for the prisoner and contrasted with the clear, straightforward manner in which Sir Francis Hopkins had given his testimony.

The Chief Baron summed up the evidence and the jury retired at about nine o'clock to consider their verdict.

The Lordships remained in court until half past ten that evening and then, hearing that there was no probability on an early finding, had bailiffs sworn to guard the doors, so as to prevent egress or ingress to the jury and postponed the court until eight o'clock the following morning, at which hour, they promised attendance should the jury have agreed a verdict.

Chapter 5

The First Jury and What Happened Next

Westmeath Guardian **Report 22 January 1846**

The jury returned to the court for the third time and submitted the issue paper without finding agreement on any of the charges.

Mr Lewis, the foreman stated, "there was not the smallest probability of the jury agreeing a verdict. We stand in the same position as when we first entered the jury room, being ten for finding a verdict of guilty and two against it. We ask your lordships for a discharge. We are exhausted after sitting and fasting for about 36 hours; we are in much need of rest and refreshment. Two of the jury members are very ill and unable to continue any longer without extreme danger to their health. I am talking about Mr Dawson and Mr Maxton. The two gentlemen in question stated their inability to continue on the jury without imminent danger to their lives."

The Chief Justice enquired as to what doctor they wished to consult as, by law, they must be certified by a medical doctor as to their inability to continue as members of the jury.

Both men selected Dr Middleton however, approximately an hour had elapsed before it was discovered that he was unavailable. Dr Stokes was then sent for and on arrival at the courthouse, he examined the individuals in question. He pronounced on oath that he believed Mr Dawson was medically unfit to safely continue on the jury: his pulse was up to 125 and he was quite feverish. Dr Stokes also certified Mr Maxton as unfit to continue as a member of the jury, adding that he was suffering from a bout of depression. At approximately 8.30pm, the judge discharged the jury without their finding any verdict.

The Attorney General announced that, in fairness to the prisoner and those concerned for him, he would, the next morning if so advised, place the prisoner again on trial.

Mr Gorman, for the Defence, admitted the right of the Crown to do so but would hope that they would not adopt that course.

Mr Murphy said he would read an affidavit for the Defence and he was sure it would induce the court to postpone proceedings until the next assizes.

The Attorney General replied that if the object of the learned counsel were merely to postpone the case to the following morning, he would not oppose the application but, if a longer postponement were required, he would object to it.

Mr Murphy observed that he was sure the court would say it was a case that should be postponed until next assizes.

Mr Gunning, also for the Defence, discussed the situation with the prisoner, to whom he read the affidavit, which he, Seery had made. He then appeared with the prisoner when the oath was administered to him and Mr Gunning who also swore an affidavit. Both men asserted that the contents of the respective affidavits were true.

Mr Murphy then read Seery's and Mr Gunning's affidavits to the court in order to induce them to grant a postponement of the case. Mr Gunning's affidavit contained the following:

1. When the prisoner was first arraigned, he entered at once upon his defence without making any application for a postponement.
2. The jury that tried Brian Seery were occupied in the trial for eight hours and in subsequent deliberation for 28 hours yet, they could not arrive at a conclusion and were therefore discharged.
3. The proceedings about to be taken by the Crown was, according to his knowledge and experience, altogether novel, unusual and without precedent.
4. The proceedings were likely to increase the excitement that prevailed and prevent a calm and dispassionate investigation of a case involving the life of the prisoner, and that the trial of the prisoner a second time in such precipitate haste, before the public mind was restored to tranquillity, would be injurious to the prisoner.
5. There would be no detriment to the Crown or to the public to postpone the trial until the next assizes (six weeks).
6. He did not make the affidavit for the purpose of delay.
7. The declaration made by one of the jury – that ten of them were for conviction and only two for acquittal – was likely to prejudice the public mind and prevent the prisoner from obtaining a fair and impartial trial.

Brian Seery's affidavit was to the same effect. Under these circumstances, he (Mr Murphy) hoped the court would postpone the trial.

The Attorney General said, in reply, that when his learned friend first intimated his intention of applying for a postponement of the trial, he at once expressed his readiness to allow it to stand for a day but, he now felt it to be his duty to oppose the application for a postponement until the next assizes. The learned gentleman then read the affidavit of Mr Gunning, paragraph by paragraph and observed that, he was not aware of any rule of law that made it necessary that, a trial on which a jury disagreed should be postponed from one assizes or commission to another assizes or commission.

It was plain that Mr Gunning did not think that any excitement prevailed before his client was tried that would prejudice his case otherwise, he would have applied to postpone the case. With regard to the proceeding being without precedent, he begged to say that, in this very county, a prisoner who was charged with a Whiteboy offence was again put upon his trial, the very morning after the day upon which the jury who first tried him were discharged in consequence of their non-agreement and, in the county of Kilkenny, a similar occurrence took place. With reference to the statement of existing excitement, how could it be argued that what was not an extraordinary circumstance would now cause excitement and prevent an impartial investigation?

~

My observations:

This is untrue as, when Mr Murphy opened the case for the Defence he said:

The time was unexpected and had the trial taken place at the ordinary time, when no prejudice or excitement prevailed on the subject, he would rely on a verdict at once for the prisoner.

The Crown did not contradict or object to this.

~

With regard to a postponement of the case to the next assizes, as that was a Special Commission issued for the trial of very serious offences, he (the Attorney General) did not consider himself warranted in consenting to an adjournment of the case until the next assizes. Mr Gunning had referred to the declaration of one of the jurors but, he did not know that he was warranted in the imputation that he had made of irregularity in that respect. In any event, the Crown was not responsible for the statement of a juror but, the declaration having been made, he was at a loss to understand how the effect apprehended by Mr Gunning – namely prejudicing the public mind – could be removed or prevented by the postponement of the case. Upon the part of the Crown, representing the Crown and the public, he considered that he was duty bound to oppose the application.

Mr Curran, for the Defence, addressed some observations to the court, in which he impressed upon their Lordships the propriety and mercy of consenting to the required postponement of the trial.

The Chief Justice, having consulted with the Chief Baron, who fully agreed in opinion with him, decided upon refusing the application. He said that a party was put upon his trial on a remarkable occasion, by a very eminent and highly constitutional judge, the day after a jury had disagreed with regard to his guilt and the question as to the legality of such a course had been set at rest by the highest authority in the land.

A course very similar to the present having been proposed to be taken at the Special Commission, which occurred in Cork in the year 1829. The learned judge who presided, submitted to the twelve judges two questions. Firstly, whether a jury discharged under circumstances resembling what had occurred on the present occasion – namely, the illness of a juror and the risk to his life which he would run if he were longer confined – and the judges unanimously pronounced upon the legality of that course. Secondly, whether a prisoner so situated could be put upon his trial on the following morning and to this question, the judges also gave an affirmative decision, thus declaring that both courses were perfectly legal. Under all the circumstances, the court could not grant the application.

The Attorney General went on to say that Mr Murphy, having expressed a desire that the trial should not come on until the following day, he cheerfully acceded to it. The trial was set to take place the following morning Friday 23 January 1846. (*Westmeath Guardian* report, 22 January 1846)

The Second Trial

The next morning, the following jury was empanelled:

Charles Arabin J.P., James Featherston-Haugh J.P., Toriano Lestrange J.P., W. Magil J.P., Edward Hodson J.P., S.A. Reynell J.P., William Bagnall, John Dungeon, Richard Magan, John Rochfort, Mark A. Levinge, William Perry, Esqrs.

~

As with the jury empanelled to hear the first trial, I decided to name the people selected to sit on the second jury as, these people were trusted to return a guilty verdict. I took this decision because all of the jury members were Hopkins' nearest and dearest friends. Both juries and indeed the Grand

Jury Panel were packed with Hopkins' cronies. The majority of jury members that tried Seery called to see Hopkins as soon as the alleged attack became known. Magistrates and some of their family members sat on one or both juries. One staunch loyalist family was represented on both juries. It did not surprise me to see John Rochfort listed as a jury member. Hopkins' residence is actually named in honour of this man's family. If you analyse the makeup of both juries, packed with Hopkins' friends, magistrates, their family members, loyalist families etc. it doesn't take a Sherlock Holmes to figure out the result of their deliberations in advance.

Members of the following families called to Rochfort House to see Hopkins, these people, or members of their families, were selected for jury service with the view of returning a guilty verdict: Richard Levinge, G. Levinge and Mark A. Levinge; W. Featherston and James Featherston-Haugh; and Toriano Lestrange called to see Hopkins at Rochfort House and sat on the second jury. John H. Shiel (magistrate) called to Rochfort House and sat on the first jury. R. Swift called to Rochfort House and sat on the first jury. John Hudson sat on the first jury and Edward Hudson sat on the second jury. I have no record of the Hudson's calling to Rochfort House to see Hopkins but, that doesn't mean they didn't pay him a visit. Catholic members of the Grand Jury Panel were precluded from sitting on the second jury – two Catholics sat on the first jury.

The *Westmeath Guardian* failed to publish details of the transcript or report on what took place during the second trial. The reason given was that they deemed the trial to be the same as the report on the first trial. Unbelievably, a week later, this newspaper republished their report on the first trial together with a small number of alterations. I know the second trial lasted the entire day however, this Tory newspaper saw fit to publish a tiny percentage of the proceedings. I don't know everything that occurred during the second trial except that Brian Seery was convicted, sentenced to death and later executed. I also know the prison chaplain, Father Savage, accused Sir Francis Hopkins of changing his evidence, thereby perjuring himself, at one of the trials. Unfortunately, I was unable to discover what evidence Father Savage was talking about.

I know Sir Francis Hopkins was cross-examined about the first time he saw the prisoner after the attack and he answered,

> *Seery was coming to Rochfort on a car between two policemen. I was sitting in a room, the window of which commanded a view of the drive to the house.*

On another occasion he said:

The first time I saw Seery after the attack was in the hall of Rochfort House.

When questioned about this, he justified the contradiction by stating that he supposed Mr Murphy's question related to the first time he saw Seery to speak to him. The question put to Hopkins was, "when did you first see Seery after the attack?" He wasn't asked "when did you first speak to Seery after the attack." Furthermore, Hopkins didn't speak to Seery when he saw him in the hall of Rochfort House, so what was he on about?

There is a contradiction as to where Seery was when Hopkins first saw him after the alleged attack. There was no contradiction about the time he said saw the coat.

Hopkins added:

Constable Johnston was the first who showed me the coat at five o'clock the following day.

This, of course, was Thursday, the day Mrs Kiernan said the police took Seery's coat from her home. So, how could the coat be found at the alleged crime scene on Wednesday morning?

With regard to the omission of Seery's name in the first information, he said he thought it was a very grave omission, adding that it was not his job to teach the Government Magistrate, who earned £600 a year. He then went on to insult Mr French, simply because this gentleman, an honest magistrate, told the truth. Of course, Hopkins, a dishonest rogue, did what dishonest rogues do when cornered and under pressure – he lied.

Hopkins failed to inform the court that, before signing, he had read the first statement and was very satisfied with the content. If he wasn't satisfied with what was enshrined in the statement, why would he sign on the dotted line? He also failed to mention the fact that, before he (Hopkins) read the statement, Mr French read it aloud in the presence of two magistrates, who also certified the written statement as correct and right. Dr Ferguson was also present so, with the exception of Mr French, we have four educated individuals present, this includes Hopkins and not one mentioned the fact that Seery's name was omitted from the document.

During the second trial, the Prosecution introduced a number of new witnesses. They were members of the gentry and very close friends with Hopkins. These gentlemen were amongst the first people to call out to Rochfort House, to see Hopkins after news of the attack became known. Among the new witnesses to give evidence was J.C. Lyons. He was one of the magistrates who certified Hopkins first statement, written by Mr French, as being a true and accurate recording of what Sir Francis Hopkins said.

Lyons, altered his story in court when he stated:

> *The informations did not contain all that Sir Francis Hopkins said about the attack, as he had named the person who had tried to kill him and, this was omitted.*

(The *Westmeath Guardian* published snippets from the second trial in an attempt to support Hopkins but, omitted to mention blatant contradictory evidence).

Lyons said nothing about the omission of the coat or hat and why Hopkins also said in his first statement that:

> *I was attacked by two unknown assailants and would recognise one of them if I saw him again.*

The thing is, if Lyons knew what Hopkins said he knew, why did he sign the informations and why didn't he give this evidence during the first trial?

Mr William Reilly was the second magistrate who certified Hopkins' first informations, as taken down by Mr French, as being a true and accurate recording of what had transpired between Hopkins and Mr French. These gentlemen must have deemed everything to be in order at that time, or they would have voiced an opinion one way or another. It beggars belief that four intelligent men, Hopkins, Lyons, Reilly and Ferguson were in attendance throughout the entire time and not one of them noticed anything awry with the proceedings.

Another new witness, Mr F. Uniacke, a close friend of Hopkins, actually let him down when he stated:

> *I was not at Rochfort before the first information was taken.*

Hopkins wrote to the editor of the *Freeman's Journal*. The letter, dated 17 February (four days after Seery's execution) is as follows:

> *Mr French must have forgotten that at Rochfort, on the 1st of December, he admitted having heard Seery's name mentioned and assigned his reasons for not inserting it in the first informations to Mr Seed, the Crown Solicitor, in the presence of Mr Browne, his clerk. Mr Bookey, sub-inspector of constabulary in Mullingar, myself, and others. From these gentlemen, I have letters stating their perfect recollection of this fact. The public can now fairly judge between Mr French's testimony and my own.*

None of the above men were witness to what Hopkins said while giving his statement to Mr French, and French denied their version of events on that December day.

Hopkins is now reduced to grasping at straws. First of all, why weren't these letters produced in court? The simple fact is, most of them were not written until after Seery's execution. I've read some of the letters; the writers contradict some of Hopkins evidence and some of his friends even contradict themselves but that didn't matter – their written evidence was not sworn evidence. Two of Hopkins' letter writers actually signed the first statement as being a true and accurate recording of what had been said, when Mr French read that statement aloud.

> *Mr Seed, the Crown Solicitor* (the man who admitted, in a letter to Dublin Castle, that he had a word with members of the Grand Jury prior to the commencement of the second trial), *in that letter he wrote the following, "I beg to state that I have had an opportunity of conversing with many of the Grand Jurors at present assembled here on the subject of the Commission (special assizes) and they all seem to be very well satisfied, and I think it will very probably be the means of restoring tranquillity to the county."*

One would imagine the author of the above, if he really knew what Hopkins alleged he knew, would definitely have taken the stand during both trials, in an attempt to copper-fasten the Crown case. This man would have no problem whatsoever giving such evidence to any court of law in an attempt to murder an innocent Irishman. As far as Mr Seed was concerned, Brian Seery was trash simply because he was Irish and a devout Catholic. But then again, Mr Seed was not in attendance while Hopkins gave his first statement to Mr French.

Another man mentioned in Hopkins letter was Mr Bookey, Sub Inspector of Constabulary in Mullingar. Bookey (he was not present when the first statement was given by Hopkins) and his police officers would do anything in their power, legal or illegal, to secure a conviction. I have no doubt that this man, if asked by Hopkins, would have given the required evidence in support of Hopkins, who was a local magistrate and very close friend. Hopkins said there were other people in his house when he alleged that French admitted having heard Seery's name mentioned. That's all very well but, the fact is, Hopkins didn't mention Seery's name while giving his statement to Mr French.

I can't understand how the prosecution team had problems with some of the defence witness evidence, particularly the evidence of the Kiernan family and, at the same time, have no problem whatsoever with Hopkins unbelievable account, as enshrined in his statements and indeed, his evidence, and the evidence of his witnesses during the trials. This man asked to make a second statement in order to pervert the course of justice. Don't get me wrong, I have absolutely no problem with Hopkins volunteering a second statement, provided he added something he had earlier forgotten about but, to change some of the evidence is a different kettle of fish. The change was very significant: he altered,

> *I was attacked by two unknown assailants. I could recognise one of them if I saw him again*

to read,

> *I was attacked by Brian Seery and another assailant.*

The next witness for the Crown was Mr F. Mahony Esq., civil engineer. This man stated that:

> *The distance from Kiernan's house to Rochfort was eight miles by road and three-and-a-half miles and sixty perches across the lake in a straight direction.*

Another Crown witness, Head Constable Clogher, stated:

> *I rowed across the lake in 30 minutes.*

Lilliput shore is nearer to Kiernan's house than Dysart shore and is, more than likely, where this police officer commenced his venture to cross the lake. I don't believe his times simply because, after running out of petrol, it took me about 40 minutes to row a little more than half that distance on a calm lake. In order to row an old heavy timber boat from Lilliput to Belvedere Shore in 30 minutes, I believe one would need to be an Olympic standard rower.

The fact is, the Prosecution team realised there was no way Seery could travel to and from Hopkins' house by road and have enough time to do what they accused him of doing. So, what did they do? They invented this 'crossing the lake theory'. However, the inventers of this scenario were unable to locate a boat berthed on either Lilliput or Dysart shore on the night in question. These people failed miserably as they attempted to prove that Seery rowed across the lake. They also knew that, for Seery to walk to Rochfort House and back to the Kiernan residence in Dysart area was definitely out of the question.

Taking everything into consideration, there is no way Seery would have enough time to do all he was convicted of doing. The alleged attack occurred about midnight. Seery would have great difficulty sneaking unnoticed out of Kiernan's house before midnight: it's very doubtful if everyone in the house was asleep at that time. To set up an alibi, Seery would have to be back in Kiernan's before anyone was awake and up out of bed. However, there was no way Seery could have been "laying in wait" outside Hopkins' house from somewhere between 11.30pm and 1.00am. The Prosecution alleged that the attackers lay in wait. For how long, they didn't say. Think about it – this "laying in wait" allegation doesn't make sense, for the simple reason that Seery, or any local labourer, would know anything about Hopkins' social life; they wouldn't know if he was at home, out partying or whatever.

During the second trial, the Prosecution cross-examined Mrs Elizabeth Kiernan. This lady was verbally attacked and accused of lying to the court as she gave her evidence during the first trial. The Attorney General's behaviour towards this lady was nothing short of criminal. This man twisted her previous evidence and put it to her that she told a different story during the first trial. He convinced the jury members (not that they needed any convincing) that Mrs Kiernan stated, "she locked the hall door on the night of the alleged attack" and added, her daughter, Catherine, swore that it was she who locked the door. The Attorney General put it to her that the two of them didn't lock the door. The fact is (and I quote from the Tory newspaper) the *Westmeath Guardian* published a report on the first trial:

> *Mrs Elizabeth Kiernan, when questioned by Mr Gorman, stated, "He (Seery) went out with John Kiernan (her son) to see the cattle. I went to bed and left the family at the fire. I was up first in the house that morning and he (Seery) and John Kiernan very soon came downstairs. The door was not unlocked until my son and the prisoner came down."*

Cross-examined by the Attorney General during the first trial, Mrs Kiernan said:

> *I could not say what time he (Seery) quit digging; he dug until dark. The doors are locked every night. The prisoner and his man (Myles Dalton), Michael Finn (my servant boy) and my own family were all there that Monday night.*

At no time did Mrs Kiernan state that she locked a door on the nights (Monday and Tuesday) in question. These people didn't care; they just made it up as they went along. They knew, as long as they had the jury "packed" with bloodthirsty loyalists, they could say and do as they pleased. At that time, the British judiciary were famous for this type of behaviour.

Her daughter, Catherine, cross-examined by Mr Clarke stated:

> *I saw Seery go to his room that Tuesday night and shut the door after him. I was standing on the lobby at the time. I always locked the hall door and left the key in.*

To a juror she said:

> *I locked the hall door on Monday and Tuesday and left the key in it. I think the prisoner could not get out. My mother never locks it unless I am away from home.*

The Attorney General next turned to Mrs Kiernan's evidence concerning her son, John. He said that her account of her son not being at dinner on Monday, although sending for him, was at variance with her son's evidence that he came home on Monday, as usual, without being sent for and dined in the kitchen with the men.

Once again, I take my information from the Tory newspaper's published report on the first trial:

> *Mrs Kiernan swore that, "On Monday night, both Seery and John Kiernan had cold meat for supper, as they did not come home for dinner. I sent out for John but, he was looking after the cattle and could not come in. Bacon and cold goose was what they had."*

Re-examined by Mr Murphy, Mrs Kiernan said:

> *The men quit at the usual time for working. The persons in the house were: Myles Dalton, Mick Finn, Brian Seery, John Kiernan, my three daughters and John Burns.*

Her son John said:

> *I dined at home that Monday in the kitchen, came home without being sent for by my mother. Myles Dalton, John McDonnell, Michael Finn, John Burns, Brian Seery and myself dined together.*

While John did state his mother did not send for him on the Monday, he never said he came home as usual on the Monday. He never said he was in time for dinner. He never mentioned dinner. What he did say was, "I dined."

Mrs Kiernan never said that John and Seery dined on their own on that Monday night. She said, "the men quit at the usual time for working." She then named all who were in the house at the time."

I can't understand the need to twist the evidence, especially when a man's life is at stake. The issue of sending for someone to come home for dinner is miles away from the real world. When I realised that the Attorney

General treated this as significant, I decided to put it to the test. Mrs Kiernan gave her statement two days after the alleged Tuesday night attack. They were talking about Monday night so, that gave me a time factor of three days with which to work. I approached five mothers and asked the following questions: Three days ago, did you call your kids in for dinner? Did they come home themselves or were they actually in the house when dinner was being served?

One of the ladies stated, "As far as I can remember", the others couldn't say one way or the other. The ladies gave a number of reasons for this but, the most common excuse was, 'It's very difficult being a mother. A mother is overburdened with housework, between cooking, making beds, cleaning the house etc. it's just impossible to remember.'

Household chores were more difficult over 170 years ago. You might say, there were two adult daughters in the Kiernan family home and that's true. However, they also worked on the farm and, as their father was away, his work still had to be done.

Mrs Kiernan, who was described by some newspapers as an old lady, would have been at least forty years older than the above five ladies. It's only natural for people to forget recent events as they grow older: it's all part of the aging process. So, it's easy to understand why there was a discrepancy between Mrs Kiernan's evidence and her sons. This discrepancy, in any right-thinking juror's mind, would be so insignificant that, they would be too embarrassed to mention it during deliberations. Having said that, it could have been that her son, John, who was mistaken and, his mother did send for him. However, I'll say this, the line of questioning should have been geared at establishing whether or not Brian Seery was eight miles away in Kiernan's house at the time of the alleged attack at Rochfort House. What the witnesses ate at mealtimes, or what time people arrived home for dinner or, if they were called for dinner has, in my opinion, no bearing on the case whatsoever.

The Attorney General lied and cheated in order to murder an innocent man. So, what's new? These people have been lying, robbing and plundering from the time they arrived in this country, right up until they left twenty-six of our counties, in December 1922. They mugged us, threw us off our land and left us living in ditches. Their behaviour, at that time, was tantamount to what I would call skulmuggery. They were also involved in skulthuggery and skulbuggery, not to mention skulduggery. Three of these words are not in the English dictionary but, I think they should be as, in my opinion, they describe perfectly the conduct of the British authorities throughout their occupation of Ireland.

The trial and indeed the story emanating from the fabulist, Sir Francis Hopkins, the day after the alleged attack and relayed to the media by the authorities contains so many discrepancies and indeed, far-fetched claims that, they deserve a place in "The Fairy Tales of Ireland". Two months later, he actually repeated the fable as he gave evidence during Seery's trials. The unbelievable heroics of the "Bad Bart" – as described by the man himself, the Prosecution and the media – was the type of fantasy character future film writers have dreamed of coming up with. Hollywood, many years later, repackaged and renamed the character. Yes, you guessed it, it seems "Superman" originated in Mullingar from the "Fairy Tales of Hopkins".

The newspapers stated that the "villain lodged about eighteen bullets and slugs of various sizes in the door immediately adjoining where Hopkins stood." This man must have been a blind villain. While in possession of a blunderbuss, he allegedly fired and missed a fully-grown man standing a few yards away. Without a doubt, Hopkins, in this instance, would have been the proverbial "sitting duck".

An article that appeared in the *Westmeath Guardian*, published two days after the alleged attack, stated that the super Sir,

> *... sprang to grapple the assailants and succeeded in clutching one – the one with the gun with whom he had a struggle. He believed that he would have secured this man but, the second man pushed his pistol at the breast of Sir Francis and drew the trigger, adding, "the gun misfired only burning priming."*
> *Sir Francis threw himself at the second man with such violence that they both fell to the ground. At this stage, he was overmatched by the two ruffians and cried for help.*

That's the story Hopkins told everybody and anybody who would listen to him and, of course, the Tory newspaper was delighted to run with it. We are talking about two armed men being beaten and badly beaten by a man returning from a party, who no doubt was drunk. In actual fact, the man would need to be out of his mind from the effects of alcohol to take on two armed, would-be assassins.

The story about the pistol misfiring and only burning primer, as it was held to Hopkins breast, just didn't happen simply because, there were no gunpowder burns on his clothing. Two months later, Hopkins realised this may be questioned so, he decided on paper to amend his story and move the pistol to "about two feet" from his breast. However, at two feet away, evidence of the burned gunpowder would still show up on his clothing.

Another thing that I can't understand is, why Seery was charged and convicted for attacking Hopkins with a gun and a pistol, where Hopkins said that the second man used the pistol.

The Attorney General also stated that Hopkins was "perfectly sober". I don't believe that for one minute. Hopkins said that he got out of the carriage himself and I believe he did: for the simple reason that he was drunk. Normally, the likes of Hopkins would never open the door and as he said, "let myself down from the carriage." People of his stamp do absolutely nothing for themselves, let alone open the carriage door. That simple procedure would be foreign to the likes of him.

Officially, not one of the guests attending the party at Colonel Caulfield's residence were questioned, despite the fact that Hopkins admitted there were at least 20 guests in attendance. I have a feeling they were questioned: this is normal police procedure as they search for evidence to support every prosecution case. Individuals who may have information are always approached and questioned by the authorities. If the party goers made statements that were deemed to be unhelpful to the Crown case (this often happened), the statements would simply be set aside. I have a feeling that some of the partygoers stated that Hopkins was drunk, and if so, did he fall as he left the party? Did they lift him into the carriage? There has to be some reason as to why the authorities decided not to use these people, it looks like their evidence would only hinder the prosecution case. The main objective of the British was to put the frighteners on the locals by murdering the unfortunate Brian Seery. Honest witnesses, people who would not change or make up stories to assist the prosecution case, were deemed to be troublesome and simply cast aside.

The Attorney General mostly agreed with the media as he reiterated, almost word for word, everything that was published in the newspapers. We have to accept that the Attorney General also believed the first assailant to be blind, because he too stated that a gun was fired, which was definitely an attempt to murder Hopkins. Adding that its contents (18 bullets and slugs) missed the target and lodged in the hall door close to where Hopkins was standing. He also put Hopkins in the Superman class when he stated,

Sir Francis appeared to be a man possessing great courage for, he at once pursued the assailant and seized him and a struggle ensued between them for the gun.

Hopkins stated:

I had just walked up the steps and pulled the bell when, I heard the shot. The man ran away. I followed him about 35 yards when I fell and, the man fell too. I caught hold of him. He had the gun in his hand.

> *Failing to take the gun off him, I caught him by the neck and throttled him.*

He went on to say:

> *I recognised him as Seery and, to leave no doubt in my mind, I forced his head up to take his profile to satisfy myself that Seery was the person.*

He continued:

> *I looked over my shoulder and saw the second man running towards me. I let Seery go and advanced towards the man when, within two feet of me, he pulled the trigger but, the pistol misfired. I dealt him a severe blow with my left hand and knocked him down.*

That's all very well however, Hopkins said he was struggling with Seery and couldn't take the gun off him. So, how was he able to get up off Seery and tackle the second man? Surely, the first attacker had a grip of Hopkins, thereby leaving it very difficult to simply 'get up off him'.

There is another problem here if what Hopkins stated was true. He said that:

> *I forced his head to take his profile to satisfy myself it was Seery.*

Wouldn't he need two hands to perform this procedure? However, let us say that he forced the attackers head using one hand. We now have the attacker with at least one free hand holding a gun. What do you think a man intent on murder, while holding an empty gun, would do to the victim? He no doubt would batter him to death.

Hopkins continued:

> *I looked around and saw the first man come with the gun, with the muzzle in his hand, in the attitude to strike me. I seized him and was struggling with him when the man with the pistol came and struck me, and brought me down on one knee. He repeated his blows five or six times. I cried for help and, the hall door being opened and light appearing from it, the two attackers ran off as fast as they could.*

It's very strange that Hopkins received no defensive wounds to his arms. Also, his knuckles should have displayed some sort of evidence that they delivered such powerful punches, capable of knocking a man to the ground.

Hopkins added:

Seery had no hat on him when I seized him. The hat which he often wore was a peculiar one. I saw the hat the following morning.

That's not what he told Dr Ferguson a few hours after the alleged attack. He told Dr Ferguson that: *"during the scuffle the fellows hat came off."* (See *Chapter 8*)

Hopkins also stated:

I attempted to disarm Seery and, failing to do so, grabbed his neck and throttled him.

He didn't say whether he used one or both hands. The natural thing to do would be to use both hands. However, this again would leave the "assailant" with one or two hands free and, in possession of an unloaded gun. Let's face it, a killer, or indeed anybody else being throttled while his hands are free and in possession of an unloaded gun, would certainly use it as a cudgel. With all his power, he would do his utmost to smash Hopkins' skull, thereby completing the task he allegedly set out to achieve in the first place. If you believe him, then that's the second opportunity Hopkins gave the "assailants" to get the upper hand and the attackers failed to take advantage.

After suffering this "horrific beating" from Hopkins, one would imagine Seery would be left with bruises all over his body. Certainly, his neck would display evidence corroborating Hopkins' claim, however, there wasn't a mark on his body. Reading through Hopkins evidence, one does not need to stretch one's imagination too far to come to the conclusion that he was drunk. He more than likely fell while leaving the party and, fell again getting out of the carriage or, climbing the steps as he attempted to enter his house, banging his head in the process. Of course, this sort of thing would not go down too well for a Baronet who was also a magistrate. So, he decides to hatch a story. He briefed his servants and alerted the police and doctor and anyone else who would listen to him.

Without a doubt, Hopkins was very satisfied with the content of his first statement simply because, he read and signed it. There are other issues I noticed in the prosecution witness statements that weren't explored by the Defence or the media. I am talking about the fact that Hopkins initially said,

I was attacked by two unknown assailants and I'd recognise one of them if I saw him again.

During the first trial, the Defence questioned him about the fact that Seery's name was not mentioned in the first statement. However, they never mentioned that, while giving the first statement, Hopkins told Mr French that he was attacked by two unknown assailants.

He should have been questioned on this, especially as this was certified as correct by two magistrates, Lyons and Reilly, in the presence of Dr Ferguson. Then again, maybe they did query this during the second trial and, as the local Tory newspaper decided not to publish anything that would point to Seery's innocence, we'll never know.

Dr Ferguson's evidence should have been questioned. He had said in court that:

> *It was he who mentioned Seery's name to the police and his*
> *information instigated the search for Seery.*

So, now we have two people taking the credit for instigating Seery's arrest – Hopkins and Ferguson. Ferguson was present while Hopkins gave his statement to Mr French. He also witnessed Mr French read aloud the content of the statement. He never said Hopkins mentioned Seery's name to French while giving the statement. However, before Mr French arrived, Hopkins thought about it and mentioned Seery's name to a number of magistrates. He said that he suspected Seery might be involved; he never said he recognised him. He was feeling them out to see what reaction he would get (just like a typical government leak from Dáil Éireann).

When Mr French arrived at Rochfort House, a number of magistrates mentioned to him that Hopkins "suspected" Seery was the attacker. However, as far as Mr French was concerned, this was hearsay because Hopkins didn't mention any name to him. After giving his statement, Hopkins returned to the library where the magistrates were discussing the attack. He received the encouragement he hoped for from his friends. There and then, he was sure he could get rid of Seery and save himself a year's rent in the process. Suddenly, the suspicion of Seery's involvement changed to a positive I.D. The "Bad Bart's" brain was working overtime at this stage and he immediately set the wheels in motion to rectify the Seery problem – and, at the same time, hold on to his money. He immediately volunteered a second statement. In other words, he asked for a second bite at the cherry and the rest is history.

Incidentally, there is no mention of the coat or hat in either statement. The reason for that was the fact that Seery's coat was eight miles away in the Kiernan's house. It was removed by the police after his arrest. Seery's hat was never in the hands of the police because, he left it at Pat Donohue's farm the previous May.

When the authorities finally produced a hat, it wasn't Seery's – it was tailored to look just like it. The hat itself was not mentioned in police statements until six days after the alleged attack so, I believe it took them six days to come up with a similar looking hat. Seery hadn't worn that type of hat for months prior to the alleged attack. This was unintentionally verified by a number of police officers who swore that they hadn't seen the defendant wearing the hat since the summer. The Defence produced Seery's hat during the trial but, it made no difference. At the end of the day, Hopkins achieved his aim and, with Seery out of the way, he decided his part of the deal became null and void. This man saved a year's rent at the cost of an innocent man's life.

~

William Pallinger, Hopkins' coachman agreed with his master's evidence concerning the fact that a shot was fired.

He said that he saw two men running away after he heard the shot. He saw Hopkins follow them. He got down off the coach as quickly as he could and pulled the doorbell. He then ran to his master's assistance. The men were out of sight when he reached him, Hopkins was getting up and he helped him.

~

That's all very well but, it seems very strange that the door wasn't opened before Pallinger managed to calm the horse, dismount, run to and climb the steps. After all, his master stated that he had pulled the doorbell a number of times, a couple of minutes prior to this.

It was also alleged that a shot was fired, discharging 18 slugs/bullets into the door, the bang of the gun and the slugs crashing into the door being loud enough to frighten the horse. The horse kicked up a racket. This, together with everything else, would have certainly alerted the household staff. After all they expected Hopkins home at any minute and would have been listening out for him. It's also strange that Pallinger didn't see the struggles as described by Hopkins. If he did, he failed mention anything of that nature.

~

He also said:

He saw two men running towards him. One of the attackers tripped and fell, the other came on and fired a shot. He had not quite turned the carriage when the shot was fired. The men ran away and his master followed.

~

However, Hopkins said that the man fell "after" the shot was fired. Hopkins also said that Pallinger was at Rochfort for about two months at the time. The coachman's evidence tells us that he got a good look at the attackers and, as Hopkins said, "It was a dusk night like twilight."

Pallinger would have seen Seery at Rochfort House prior to this. The Bad Bart said that Seery was there during the months of September and October. Pallinger was employed there during that time so, why didn't he recognise Seery?

~

Matthew Rogers, Steward to Hopkins, said:

> *I found a coat and tobacco pipe the following morning. I gave the coat to Mr Bookey. I was shown the hat the following morning by Thomas Telling. I found the coat about 40 yards from the house, at seven o'clock on the morning after my master was attacked.*

Thomas Telling, an employee of Hopkins stated:

> *I found a hat close to where Sir Francis was. I gave the hat to Mr Rogers,* (Rogers said that Telling showed him the hat the following morning). *Sir Francis was standing at the time I reached him and the assailants were gone. I found the hat and my master a little after the shot was fired. It was about 12 o'clock at night. It might be a quarter of an hour before or after it.*

~

This is very strange: if he found the hat and his master shortly after the shot was fired, isn't it only natural that he would have given, or at least shown the hat to Hopkins straight away?

Hopkins stated that he didn't see the hat until the next morning. So, according to Mr Telling, the finding of the hat took place in Hopkins presence and shortly after the alleged attack however, Hopkins mentioned nothing about it in either of his statements.

Mr Telling also stated, "I gave the hat to Mr Matthew Rogers," however, Hopkins said in court that "Mr Telling gave him the hat the next morning." So, who gave the hat to Hopkins? That is, if a hat existed at that time?

Telling also said that he found the hat and his master,

> *... a little after the shot was fired.*

So, he heard the "shot" and immediately went to his master's assistance. This doesn't tie in with either Hopkins' or Pallinger's evidence.

Hopkins said that at the end of the struggle, he cried for assistance and the hall door was opened.

Pallinger said:

> *After he controlled the horse, he got down off the carriage as quick as he could and pulled the bell. He then ran to assist his master.*

Pallinger also said:

> *The gunman was 6 or 7 yards from Hopkins when he fired the shot. The weapon discharged 18 slugs and bullets, this was no shotgun, it was a blunderbuss* (Nicknamed by old pirates and sailors as a "Deck Cleaner"). *I decided to get an approximate measurement of the spread of bullets and slugs on Hopkins door. However, I had to use a shotgun as I couldn't locate a blunderbuss. At six yards the pellet spread measured approximately nine inches, are we looking at eighteen inches for a blunderbuss. I'm beginning to think if a blind man, while in possession of a blunderbuss, heard the doorbell, he could point the weapon in that direction and hit the target.*

Incidentally, Telling didn't say Pallinger was with Hopkins shortly after the shot was fired; so, where was he?

How could an honest jury member convict Seery on the evidence produced by the Prosecution? In my opinion, every member of this jury convicted the poor man simply because they had murder on their minds. I am talking about cold-blooded murder at the behest of the Hopkins and the British authorities. A hat, a coat and a drunken man with a vested interest in Seery's conviction and elimination was their "smoking gun".

However, some prosecution witnesses couldn't make up their minds as to when the hat was found or, when Hopkins saw the hat or indeed, when and who handed it to Hopkins. During the first trial, when shown the hat by Mr Sergeant Warren for the Crown, Hopkins said,

> *It was like the hat that Seery was in the habit of wearing.*

Under cross-examination by Mr Murphy for the Defence, Hopkins said, "I saw the hat the following morning" and, "I identified it."

Another Crown witness, Constable Johnston, stated:

> *I cannot say that the present band was on the hat in the summer last or, what band was on it then.*

Adding:

> *I cannot be mistaken in the hat; it is the same hat I frequently saw*
> *Seery wear.*

~

How could this policeman hold a straight face after admitting "he didn't know what Seery's hat looked like in the summer" and, in the same sentence, he contradicts himself by saying, "I cannot be mistaken about the hat."

The police actually removed Seery's coat from the Kiernan's house after Seery's arrest so, just like the hat, it was impossible for it to have been found at the "crime scene".

The Prosecution stated that Seery "removed and more or less folded the coat. He then left it neatly on the ground."

During the fishing season, I have been on the shore of that lake at midnight on numerous occasions, especially during the "Green Peter" season[*]. However, I'm talking about March up until the second week in October in general but, the summer months in particular. The shore of the lake during the summer, never mind the second half of November, is bitterly cold at midnight. I've never witnessed a fisherman at midnight on the shore of the lake remove his coat while chatting with fellow anglers, unless he was about to get into his car.

After studying the case, I'm wondering why the Defence failed to probe the fact that an assailant, using a gun capable of discharging 18 slugs in one shot, could miss a target as large as a grown man at such a short distance. (Maybe this was queried during the second trial). I know the slugs spread as they travel through the air however, the type of gun used was a blunderbuss. This gun had a short barrel and had the appearance of a sawn-off shotgun. The blunderbuss was used in close quarter fighting and was very effective at short range. It would be impossible to miss a target at close range.

Incidentally, quite a number of the gentry in the area owned gun collections. In my opinion, Hopkins, after falling, blasted his door with a blunderbuss from his own collection in order to get out of his commitment to pay Seery's

---

[*] The Green Peter is a very popular natural fly that rises around mid-season and attracts anglers from all over Ireland and further afield to Lough Ennell in Co. Westmeath – the best wild trout lake in Europe.

rent and, at the same time, left it easier to explain away the bruises and cuts on his head.

Another problem that the Defence didn't question is, most witnesses state that the attack took place at about midnight and Hopkins stated that Dr Ferguson was the first person that he mentioned Seery's name to. Ferguson said he arrived at Rochfort House shortly before 2am – that's a gap of about two hours. It's difficult to believe that Hopkins didn't mention to the people who were present prior to the arrival of Dr Ferguson, that he recognised Seery as one of the attackers. In the real world, it's the first thing a victim of an attack would say to people who arrived at the scene.

It was also stated that the two attackers were hiding in the vicinity and, awaiting Hopkins return from his night-out. This doesn't make sense. Neither Seery, nor anyone else in his circle, would know anything about Hopkins social activities on the night in question. The only people privy to that information would be some members of Hopkins' staff and the gentry attending the party at Colonel Caulfield's residence. I'm positive, these would be the only people who would know anything about Hopkins' arrangements that night. For all that the ordinary folk knew, Hopkins may have been in bed, asleep and the "assassins" could be "laying in wait" until the cows came home. Some people might say that Hopkins went out every Tuesday night and as such, it was common knowledge. However, neither Hopkins nor any of his supporting witnesses mentioned this during the investigation or the trials. Also, the narrow, dark drive leading up to Hopkins' house was and still is, an ideal ambush site for someone hell bent on killing him. The trees would block any moonlight that may be present on the night, so much so that the carriage driver would have great difficulty seeing a few feet ahead of the horse.

We know that Brian Seery had every reason to keep Hopkins alive; he would need to be out of his mind to kill the man. Brian was very religious and probably prayed every day that no harm would come to Hopkins. This man's life meant a year's rent to Seery and his family. However, money-mad Francis Hopkins, worrying about their rental agreement, had other ideas, mainly, to "eliminate Seery". In my opinion, he didn't believe Seery would be executed. He was positive this unfortunate man would end his days in some faraway British colony.

I have pointed out numerous inconsistencies in the prosecution case and I wonder why the defence team seemed to ignore them. However, there is a good chance they noticed everything I pointed out and probably much more. As the proceedings of the second trial were not published in the newspapers, we don't know who was cross-examined and taken to task about their previous contradictory evidence.

During the first trial, Messrs Pallinger, Rogers, Telling, Matthews, Hopkins himself and the police constables contradicted one another; some even contradicted themselves. I'm sure the defence team extracted some of the truth out of these conspirators during the second trial and that's the reason the Tory newspapers refused to publish the proceedings. Lyons, Reilly and the prosecutors, Seed and Browne should have been involved in the first trial. I don't know if the four of them were called to give evidence during the second trial but, I do know Lyons appeared as a witness for Hopkins. However, I know they were all involved in an investigation into Mr French's behaviour four months later (see *Chapter 8*).

Brian Seery's Funeral

The second trial came to a conclusion at 9.30pm. The jury retired to begin their deliberations. They returned with a guilty verdict at midnight. After his summary, the judge pronounced the death sentence on Brian Seery as follows:

> *The sentence of the law is that you, Brian Seery, be taken upon a day to be hereafter named, to the common place of execution and there hang until you be dead, and the Lord have mercy on your soul.*

The Attorney General stood up and stated:

> *I'd like to remind your honour to add, "The prisoner should be buried within the precincts of the gaol."*

Brian Seery was executed on 13 February 1846. The priests in the parish pleaded with the judges to direct the authorities to hand over the remains to his family. The judges agreed and Brian was waked in his house, at the Brewery Yard, on Friday and Saturday. His remains were taken to the Chapel on Sunday at 12 noon. After the usual formalities of the funeral Mass, blessing of the clay and receiving offerings, he was placed in a hearse. The cortège moved slowly through the town, crossed over the Green Bridge and headed towards Castletown-Geoghegan via Dysart. An hour and a half elapsed before the last of the mourners had crossed the bridge. The hearse, at this stage, was more than three miles out the Dysart road. There were over 200 cars (carriages) containing shopkeepers and other respectable passengers including wealthy farmers. The cortege finally arrived at the cemetery, in the village of Castletown-Geoghegan.

Father Masterson who officiated at the graveside, addressed the mourners. He said:

> *You have now paid the last tribute of respect to the mortal remains of Brian Seery. I would ask one request and it is this, that you will now*

return to your homes and that no one will enter a public house in this village. You are aware that the hellhounds are on our trail; that they growl with impatience for our blood. The perjured spy and blood-thirsty informer are laying snares for your destruction. Let no one tempt you to speak this day an angry word; let no one hear you say you are displeased. The Lord has said, "Revenge belongs to me alone, and I will repay."

Father Masterson's address lasted more than twenty minutes. One loyalist newspaper, the *Westmeath Guardian* called it, "eloquent, pathetic and soul-stirring" adding,

... what hope can be entertained for the prosperity, the happiness of the advancement of Ireland. What fruits is such a broadcast sowing likely to produce?

I say in answer to that, what did the murder of Brian Seery and all the other innocent Irish people do for peace and harmony in Ireland? Well, we all know the answer."

Chapter 6

Crown Correspondence

Mr Seed to Richard Pennefather

Dublin Castle
Mullingar

January 1846

Sir,

I should have written to you before this to report the proceedings at the Special Commission but, have each day been detained in court until too late an hour to enable me to do so.

On my arrival here, I found considerable excitement prevailing with respect to some of the cases for trial. Particularly, that of Sir Francis Hopkins' case and I have no doubt that, if the necessary precautions had not been taken, some of the cases would have failed from the intimidation of and tampering with the witnesses but, I am glad to say that, with the exception of one case, we have been very successful.

The first case tried was Sir Francis Hopkins's, which I believe, in the opinion of the Attorney General and the other counsel for the Crown, was very clearly sustained by the evidence produced but the jury, after been locked up for 10 hours, could not agree and they were discharged on Tuesday evening without coming to a decision: ten being for a conviction of the prisoner and two for an acquittal.

The Attorney General, under these circumstances, has thought it right to put the prisoner on his trial a second time and, accordingly, it is intended to do so at the sitting of the court this morning, the result of which, I shall apprise you of.

The other cases tried were two for firing at the police, one for delivering a threatening notice by an armed party, one for feloniously assaulting a man of the name of Hugh Ervine and one for robbery of arms. All the latter cases resulted in the conviction of the several prisoners, with the exception of the last case, where the witness refused to swear positively to the prisoners who were, in consequence, acquitted, the Prosecution having been intimidated.

The remaining cases for trial are, one for felonious assault on a man of the name of Grennan by an armed party and one for assaulting the habitation of James Hickey and Patrick Ledwith, the result of each of which I shall report.

I beg to state that I have had an opportunity of conversing with many of the Grand Jurors at present assembled here, on the subject of the Commission and they all seem to be very well satisfied and, I think it will very probably be the means of restoring tranquillity to the county.

I shall, at the conclusion of the Commission, again take the liberty of addressing you and, on my return to town, furnish the Government with a full report of all the cases tried and,

I have the honour to be,

Sir

Your obedient Servant

Crown Solicitor

S. Seed

Mullingar January 1846

30
1581

Sir,

I should have written to you before this to report the proceedings at the Special Commission but have each day been detained in Court until too late an hour to enable me to do so.

On my arrival here I found considerable excitement prevailing with respect to some of the cases for trial, particularly that of Sir Francis Hopkins' case, and I have no doubt that if the necessary precautions had not been taken some of the cases would have failed from the intimidation of and tampering with the witnesses, but I am glad to say that with the exception of one case we have been very successful.

The first case tried was Sir Francis Hopkins' which, I believe, in the opinion of the Attorney General and the other counsel for the crown was very clearly sustained by the evidence produced, but the Jury after having been locked up for 18 hours could not agree, and they were discharged on Tuesday Evening without coming to a decision, 10 being for a conviction of the prisoner and 2 for an acquittal.

The Attorney General under these circumstances has thought it right to put the prisoner on his trial a second time and accordingly it is intended to do so at the sitting of the Court this morning, the result of which I shall apprize you of — The other cases tried were two for firing at the police

police; one for delivering a threatening Notice, by an armed party, one for feloniously assaulting a man of the name of Hugh Erwine, and one for robbery of arms; all the latter Cases resulted in the Conviction of the several prisoners, with the exception of the last case where the witness refused positively to swear to the Prisoners who were in consequence acquitted the prosecutor having been intimidated

The remaining Cases for trial are one for a felonious assault on a man of the name of Gleenian by an armed party and one for assaulting the habitation of James Hickey and Patrick Ledwith the result of each of which I shall report —

I beg to state that I have had an opportunity of conversing with many of the Grand Jurors at present assembled here on the subject of the Commission, and they all seem to be very well satisfied, and I think it will very probably be the means of restoring tranquility to the County

I shall at the conclusion of the Commission again take the liberty of addressing you and on my return to town furnish the Government with a full report of all the Cases tried and

Have the Honor to be
Sir
Your obedient Servant
S. Seed
Crown Solicitor

R. Pennyfather Esqr

Mr Seed, Crown Solicitor, correspondence, January 1846 – page 2 of 2

Transcript of Sir Francis Hopkins' letter to the Lords Chief Justices

Mullingar

Saturday, January 24, 1846

My Lord,

The sentence of death has been passed this day, upon a prisoner in the gaol of this town named Brian Seery, who has been tried and found guilty of conspiring with another person to take my life.

I now beg, respectfully, to submit to your Lordships consideration, whether by the exercise of the prerogative of mercy in this case and the substitution of some milder form of punishment, the ends of justice might not equally be obtained.

I have the honour to be,

My Lord,

Your Lordships' obedient servant

Francis Hopkins

Mullingar, Saturday Jan'y 24th
1846

My Lord,

The sentence of death has been passed this day, upon a prisoner in the gaol of this town named Bryan Seery, who has been tried and found guilty of conspiring with another person to take my life. I now beg respectfully to submit to your Lordships consideration, whether by the exercise of the prerogative of mercy in this case, and the substitution of some milder form of punishment, the Ends of Justice might not equally be obtained.

I have the honor to be
My Lord, your Lordships obedient servant
Francis Hopkins

Letter written by Sir Francis Hopkins to Lords Chief Justices

Courtesy of National Archives, Bishop Street, Dublin

Bishop Cantwell's Letter to his Excellency, the Lord Lieutenant

Mullingar

9 February 1846

My Lord,

I feel the peculiar delicacy of the subject of which I venture to address your Excellency, the office which I fill and the responsibility which it imposes will, I trust, plead my apology.

I allude to the case of Brian Seery, who is sentenced to suffer the extreme penalty of the law in this town on Friday next. I will not trespass upon your Excellency's attention by any remarks on the Special Commission, at which he was found guilty. I feel convinced that, in granting the Commission, your Excellency had no other object but to vindicate the majesty of the law to check crime by punishing guilt, to promote respect for the laws by exhibiting the evidence of their impartial administration and by preventing outrage to secure the public tranquillity.

Such, I believe, were your Excellency's benevolent object and wishes. I owe it to your Excellency; I owe it to justice; I owe it to humanity most respectfully to state my decided opinion that, towards the attainment of these blissful ends, the Commission will, in Seery's case, prove a most lamentable failure, the spirit in which it was carried out, the sectarian constitution of the jury, the foul means resorted to in order to secure it, the unimpeached excellence of Seery's character. All these circumstances combined have produced the impression on the public mind that Seery had not a fair trial and that, if executed, he will be a murdered man. I do not entertain the slightest doubt of his innocence. I do not, of course, impute blame to your Excellency or to the Law Officers of the Crown. The public are impressed with the belief that the magistrates of the county (with some few honourable exceptions) and the local officials who have for years enforced an anti-Catholic bitterness unknown in other parts of Ireland, have, in this instance, done everything in their power to secure a victim. The people feel that vengeance and not justice has been with a certain class, a leading object.

The preservation of the public peace, under the occurrences of no ordinary visitation, has been, for the last few years, a painful and difficult task with me and the clergy. The cruelties practiced and the deeds of unchristian extermination so widespread throughout this county, your Excellency could scarcely believe. If Seery be executed, I tremble for the consequences. To deprive of life and to send to a premature grave, the innocent husband of a virtuous wife and the industrious father of five helpless children, is indeed an appalling idea.

I beg, in conclusion, to assure your Excellency that in soliciting your Excellency's attention to this sad case, I am influenced perhaps, more by public consideration than by any feelings of humanity or sympathy towards Seery himself. Death will be to him, I trust in a merciful God, only the passage to a happy eternity.

John Cantwell

R. C. Bishop of Meath

Transcript of Letter from Dublin Castle to Bishop Cantwell

Dublin Castle

10 February 1846

Right Revd Sir,

I am commanded, by the Lord Lieutenant, to acknowledge the receipt of your letter of the 9th inst and to assure you that you do His Excellency but justice in yours – enumeration of the reasons which you presume led to the appointment of a Special Commission to try the several prisoners confined in the gaol in Mullingar. But, His Excellency observes, with regret, the opinion you have decided to pronounce upon the mode in which the trial of one of them, Brian Seery, was conducted and the strong expressions you make was of, in reprobative of the conduct of the magistrates and those whom you are pleased to denigrate as "Local Officials".

His Excellency has read with the deepest attention the memorials in favour of Brian Seery: the opinion of the judges to whom these memorials were referred; the reasons assigned by the Crown Solicitors for exercising the right to challenge the original informations, and the judges notes of the trial.

From all these various documents, His Excellency regrets to say, he can come to no other conclusion other than justice requires that the law should take its course.

I have the honour to be,

Right Reverend Sir,

Your very obedient humble servant

Signature: Richard Pennefather

Dublin Castle
10th February 1846

Right Revd Sir
          I am commanded by the
Lord Lieutenant to acknowledge the
receipt of your Letters of the 9th inst.,
and to assure you, that you do His
Excellency but justice in your
— enumeration of the reasons
which you presume led to the
appointment of a Special Commission
to try the several Prisoners Confined
in the Gaol of Mullingar — but
His Excellency observes with regret,
the opinion, you have deemed it
proper to pronounce, upon the mode
in which the Trial of one of them,
Bryan Seery, was conducted, in
the strong expressions you make use
of, in reprobation of the Conduct of
the Magistrates & those whom you are

The Right Revd
Bishop Cantwell

Letter from Dublin Castle to Bishop Cantwell – page 1 of 2

Courtesy of National Archives, Bishop Street, Dublin

pleased to designate as
"local Officials".

His Excellency has read
with the deepest attention the
Memorials which have been
presented in favor of Bryan
Seery — the opinion of the Judges
to whom those Memorials were
referred — the reasons assigned
by the Crown Solicitor for
exercising the right of Challenge
— the original informations — and
the Judges notes of the Trial —

From all these various
documents, His Excellency
regrets to say, He can come to
no other conclusion, than that
Justice requires, that the Law
should take its Course.

I have the honor to be
Right Reverend Sir
Your very obedient
humble Servant

Richard Pennefather

Letter from Dublin Castle to Bishop Cantwell – page 2 of 2

Transcript of Letter to Dublin Castle re: Execution of Brian Seery

Mullingar

13th February 1846

In obedience to your order of the 9th inst., I proceeded yesterday from my quarters to Mullingar in order, if necessary, to cooperate and advise with the local magistrates, as to any precautions they might deem necessary to be taken today. I met Mr French R.M. but none of the local magistrates. We waited on Sir Guy Campbell and informed him that, as with the Sheriff or any of the local magistrates, some in town, we could not say what precautionary measures might be necessary, that from information received, it appeared the R.C. clergy warned and ordered their parishioners not, on any account, to come into Mullingar on the day of Seery's execution. That trumped, all we could suggest, until the Sheriff arrived, was that the troops should parade at such hour as he deemed right.

This morning, the Sub Sheriff arrived at half past ten o'clock. I communicated with him and he sent a requisition to the General for 200 infantry to attend at the execution at 11 o'clock. The troops accordingly placed, there was scarcely a problem to be seen in the streets. The shops of the Roman Catholics have closed. ? ? ?. At 12 o'clock, Seery was taken out by the Revd. Mr Masterson and said:

"Good people, I wish you to be my witness that I am innocent and had neither hand, act, part or knowledge of the crime I am going to suffer for."

He was then brought back – he had a black crucifix in his hand when he made the declaration.

He recommenced praying again, with the Rev Mr Masterson until the 12 o'clock coach arrived from Dublin, by which, it would appear they expected a reprieve.? he went down to consequences of some declaration of his innocence ? ? ? that were understood to be taken from Seery on yesterday.

The Rev Mr Savage waited the arrival of the coach and, on finding that no reprieve had come, he went to the gaol. Immediately, the convict was brought out and executed.

After hanging, the remains of his body were placed in a coffin and taken by a few persons to his house. None of the local magistrates were in attendance.

I shall return to my station tomorrow,

Regards.

R.M.

R Pennefather

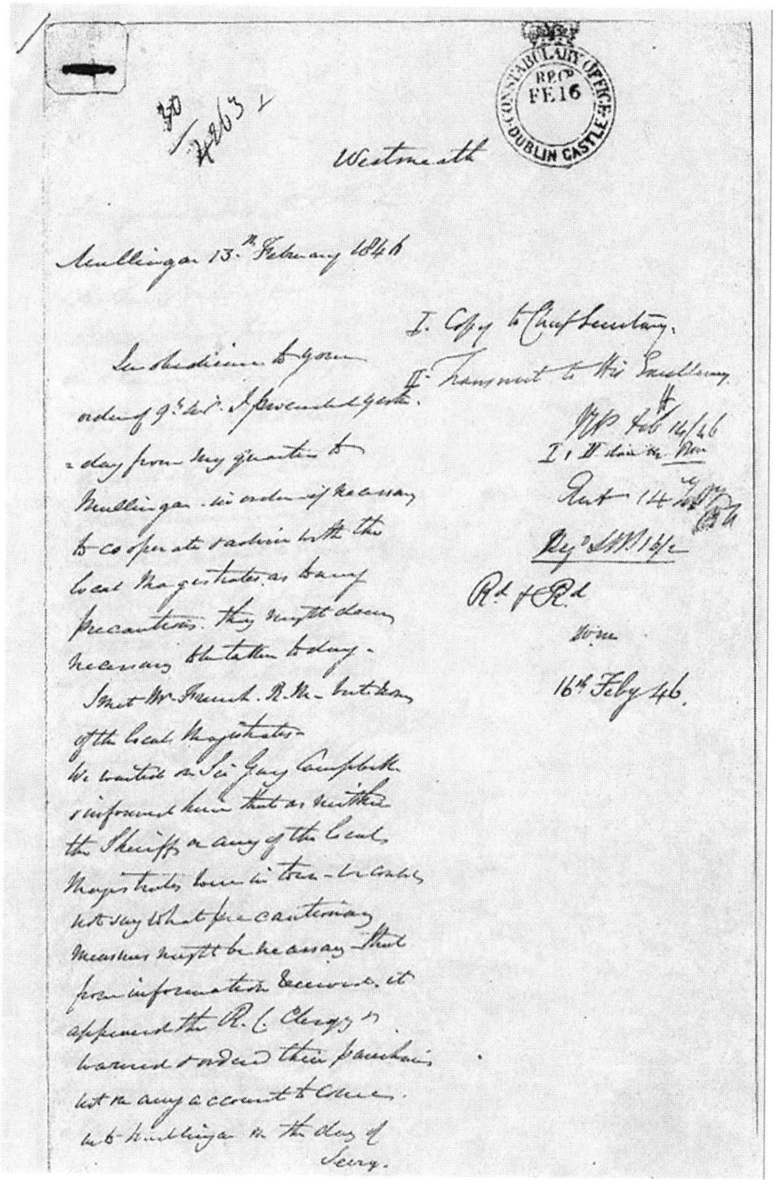

Constabulary Office Rec^d FE16 Dublin Castle

Westmeath

Mullingar 13th February 1846

I. Copy to Chief Secretary.
II. Transmit to His Excellency.
[illegible] Feb 14/46
I, II done the [illegible]
Rect 14 [illegible]
Reg^d [illegible]
R^d & R^d
[illegible]
16th Feby 46.

In obedience to your order of 9th inst. I proceeded yesterday from my quarters to Mullingar in order if necessary to co-operate and advise with the local Magistrates as to any precautions they might deem necessary to be taken today.
I met Mr French R.M. but none of the local Magistrates.
We waited on Sir Guy Campbell and informed him that as neither the Sheriff or any of the local Magistrates were in town we could not say what precautionary measures might be necessary – that from information received it appeared the R.C. Clergy had warned and ordered their parishioners not on any account to come into Mullingar on the day of Seery.

Letter to Dublin Castle re Execution of Brian Seery – page 1 of 3

Courtesy of National Archives, Bishop Street, Dublin

Seerys execution. that therefore
all be ... suggest until
the Sheriff arrived here. that
the troops should parade and ...
soon as he deemed right.

This morning the Sub Sheriff
arrived at ½ past Ten
O'clock. I communicated with
him. and he sent a requisition
to the General for 200 infantry
to attend at the Execution.
at 11 O'clock the troops accordingly
paraded. there was scarcely a person
to be seen in the streets. The Shops of
all Roman Catholics been closed.
Perfect Stillness prevailed. At
12 O'clock Seery was brought out
by the Revd Mr Marturd & said
"Good people I wish you all to know
that I am innocent. and had neither
hand, act, part or knowledge of
the crime I am going to suffer for"
he was then brought back — he had
a black crucifix in his hand.

Letter to Dublin Castle re Execution of Brian Seery – page 2 of 3

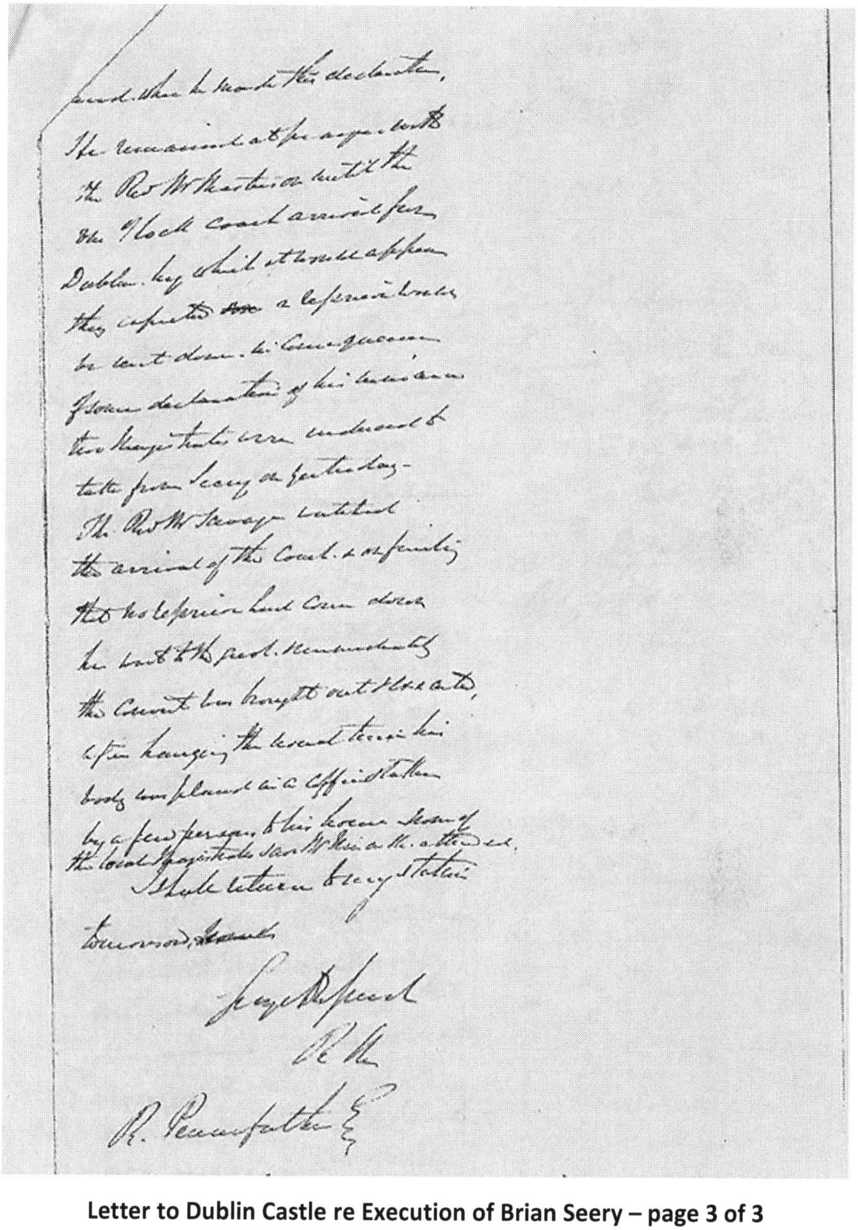
saved when he made this declaration,
He remained at prayer with
the Revd Mr Martin &c until the
9 o'clock coach arrived from
Dublin by which it would appear
they expected a reprieve would
be sent down. In consequence
of some declaration of his innocence
two Magistrates were induced to
take from Seery on yesterday –
The Revd Mr Savage watched
the arrival of the Coach & on finding
that no reprieve had come down
he went to the gaol. Immediately
the convict was brought out & executed,
after hanging the usual time his
body was placed in a coffin & taken
by a few persons to his house. Some of
the local Magistrates [illegible] attended.
I shall return to Seery's station
tomorrow, [illegible]
[illegible] Respectfully
R.M.
R. Pennefather Esq

Letter to Dublin Castle re Execution of Brian Seery – page 3 of 3

Courtesy of National Archives, Bishop Street, Dublin

Chapter 7

Letters and Newspaper Reports

~

After Seery's arrest, Sir Francis Hopkins, Bart, asked to make a second statement, this time he deleted the sentence, "I was attacked by two unknown assailants. I would recognise one of them if I saw him again." The encouragement of close friends led to his greedy brain kicking in and replaced the above with, "I was attacked by Brian Seery and another assailant."

The *Westmeath Guardian*, a Tory newspaper, interviewed both Hopkins and the police, two days after the attack, the *Guardian* published its report, one paragraph was as follows:

~

Westmeath Guardian, 20 November 1845

The police were quickly at the scene and immediately began investigating the circumstances surrounding the attack.

The writer added:

Hopkins recognised the man who fired the shot and furnished the police with the name and description of this person. Mr Bookey, Sub Inspector, lost no time in apprehending him, with the assistance of Constable Johnston of Dysart station, in whose neighbourhood the attacker was at work. On being brought to Rochfort last night, he was fully identified by Sir Francis Hopkins as the person who fired the bullet and, we also understand that the hat which the assassins left after them, has been identified as belonging to the man the police apprehended.

~

That reads very convincing except for the fact that Hopkins had changed his story and failed to mention the existence of two informations. The writer claimed it was Hopkins who gave the police Seery's name and, as a result the police lost no time in apprehending him. However, Dr Ferguson claimed it was he who "communicated Seery's name to the police" adding, "in consequence of which the prisoner was arrested." However, they failed to add that despite knowing Seery very well, Hopkins only suspected him to be one of the assailants. The reporter added, "Hopkins was still in considerable danger" while in reality, he was healthy and well enough to entertain his friends, who called to see him.

This same newspaper wrote about the "scuffle between Hopkins and Seery" yet, failed to mention the fact that there wasn't a mark on the accused's body. The writer goes on to say,

> *The assassins were worried that the coachman might sound the alarm and summon assistance from members of the household staff.*

~

The writer didn't even try to explain why the door bell, the gun blast, 18 slugs and bullets crashing into the door, an out-of-control horse yoked up to a carriage and the coachman shouting as he attempted to control the horse, all failed to alert the household staff. (Maybe the volume of their 1845 model "Ghetto Blaster" or "Television", etc. was turned up too high).

~

The Times, 27 January 1846

> *Brian Seery has been tried and convicted of the attempted murder of Sir Francis Hopkins (a resident landlord in County Westmeath, Ireland) on 18 November 1845. The great famine had begun, the country was in a state of near rebellion and the assassination attempt was thought to be the work of the Ribbonmen – a secret society of armed insurgents, primarily young Catholic tenant farmers.*

At Seery's trial, the judge commented:

> *I have seldom had cases brought before me – cases which more exhibited the dreadful scourge that, wherever it was permitted to take root, struck at the very foundation of all social order and placed in jeopardy peace and security of every individual in the country.*

~

In reality, Seery was executed, among other things, to contain the ongoing unrest in the Mullingar area.

~

The Times, 7 February 1846

There had been many concerns about Seery's conviction, as is common in trials with political implications. Most Rev Dr Cantwell, Bishop of Meath wrote to the paper noting,

> *The manner in which the commission was obtained and carried out, the unimpeached excellence of Seery's character through life, the omission to summon Catholic jurors, the sectarian arrangement of the general list, the dissent of the jury on the first trial, the exclusion by the Crown of respectable gentlemen on the second trial (to which the Crown resorted after the trifling of a day from the discharge of the first jury), the jury not having given weight to the testimony of the stipendiary magistrate, of two policemen and of six other credible and respectable witnesses, all contradicting the evidence given by the prosecutor (Hopkins) who, in a most important fact, contradicted even himself.*

~

Freeman's Journal (quoted in *The Times*, 16 February 1846)

Before he was executed, Seery issued a written statement from his cell:

> *I, Brian Seery, now a prisoner in the gaol in Mullingar and on this day to be executed, do most solemnly and sincerely declare, in the presence of that God before whom I must shortly appear for judgement, that I never fired at Sir Francis Hopkins, that I never committed any act tending to injure him in person or property and that I was never cognizant of, or a party to any conspiracy to plot or shoot or injure the said Sir Francis Hopkins, and that I am not guilty, directly or indirectly of the crime for which I am to be hanged.*
> Signed: Brian Seery

> *When the prisoner appeared on the drop, he said, raising his crucifix and in a calm, loud and steady tone, with an emphasis of awful and terrible solemnity,*

I declare before my God that I had neither act, hand, part or knowledge in the crime for which I am going to die here!

This declaration, so pronounced, caused a shudder amongst the soldiery, and the prayer, "the Lord have mercy on him", burst from every lip. A few moments more and the unhappy man was launched into eternity.

~

Letter from Sir Francis Hopkins to the Editor of the *Freeman's Journal*

Sir,

As long as the fate of Seery hung in the balance, I abstained from taking any steps that might, hereafter, be said to have the effect of turning the scale against him. But now that the law has taken its course, I deem it my duty to make a few remarks, in consequence of certain statements that have appeared in your columns and other of the public prints.

It has been stated that I solicited a commutation of the extreme punishment of death and, an inference was drawn therefrom that I had changed my mind respecting the identity of my assailant. It is true that I did solicit the clemency of the Crown for the unhappy prisoner, who, on this occasion, I believe to have been the tool of others but, I most solemnly deny that a shadow of a doubt ever crossed my mind as to the identity of my assailant and, notwithstanding the reported dying declaration of innocence by Seery on the scaffold. I again affirm that he was the person who fired at and subsequently assaulted me on the night of the eighteenth of November last and, such is my positive and unalterable conviction.

Much comment has been made of the omission of Seery's name in the first informations. I stated on oath on the trial that I had mentioned Seery's name to the stipendiary magistrate at the time he took those informations. Mr French distinctly swore that, to the best of his knowledge and belief I had not mentioned any name. Upon this, I shall make no comment further than to observe that in so doing, Mr French must have forgotten that at Rochfort on the 1st of December, he admitted having heard Seery's name mentioned and assigned his reasons for not inserting it in the first informations to Mr Seed, the Crown Solicitor, in the presence of Mr Browne, his clerk, Mr Bookey, Sub-Inspector of constabulary in Mullingar, myself and others. From these gentlemen, I have letters stating their perfect recollection of this fact.

The public can now fairly judge between Mr French's testimony and my own. I was sworn on the trial (but this fact has not been commented on in your journal) by a constable of the Dysart Police Station, distant six miles from Mullingar, that he had received a written order at five o'clock in the morning to arrest Seery. The first informations were sworn at 11am subsequently. This should satisfy most persons that the name of Seery had been mentioned before the first informations were sworn.

I am, your obedient Servant,

Francis Hopkins
Sackville Street Club – February 17, 1846

~

Hopkins, a pathological liar, wrote the following on the above date, just a few days after the execution of Brian Seery:

I abstained from taking any steps that might, hereafter, be said to have the effect of turning the scale against Seery but, now that the law has taken its course, I deem it my duty to make a few remarks, in consequence of certain statements which have appeared in your columns and other of the public prints.

~

The fact is, he lobbied every Magistrate in the county, members of the prosecution team, members of the Grand Jury and everyone he came in contact and partied with from the date of the alleged attack and, continued his lobbying even after Seery's death. Other than the above he "abstained from taking any steps that might, hereafter, be said to have the effect of turning the scale against Seery."

Is this man for real? Despite swearing in court:

I may have told this transaction fifty times but, I think not one hundred times. I have told it both before and after dinner. I told it to a great many gentlemen of the county.

He also swore that he met and briefed all the Magistrates of the county the day after the alleged attack. This liar briefed all of the above with the aim of screwing an innocent man and saving himself money.

He also wrote – in his letter to the editor of the *Freeman' Journal* – that he believed Seery to have been "the tool of others". Who or what organisation was he referring to? The problem here is, Hopkins swore in court that Seery was told to "prepare his coffin" if he took over any of the farms he showed an interest in. This leads me to believe Seery was not a member of the Whiteboys, Ribbonmen or any other republican movement.

Hopkins quoted the names of people who wrote to him and, he said that they backed his version of events alleged to have taken place on 1st December at Rochfort House. Mr Browne's name was mentioned however, he stated the following in his letter to Hopkins:

> *I do not recollect to have heard it stated, after Mr French came into the room, that Sir Francis had mentioned the name at the time of taking the first information.*

Mr Seed, Crown Solicitor, is also mentioned as a supporter of Hopkins. This is the man that lobbied members of the Grand Jury. After what happened at the first trial, he wanted to be fully sure the members of the second jury were onside and would deliver a guilty verdict.

Mr Bookey also wrote a letter of support for Hopkins. This man was the senior police officer responsible for the skulduggery that sent the unfortunate Brian Seery to an early grave.

Hopkins had some neck. He thought everyone was stupid, especially the locals. He really believed that they hadn't the intelligence to check his evidence, letters, statements, etc. However, as it transpired, he wasn't believed locally, nationally or globally. In my opinion, right now, Hopkins is a senior member, maybe the chairman of the committee in hell. Satan himself has learned a lot from the "Bad Bart", since they joined forces the day this evil man died.

~

Letter from Fr. J. Savage to the Editor of the *Freeman's Journal*

> *Dear Sir,*
>
> *I have seen in your paper of yesterday, a letter from Sir Francis Hopkins, which I consider deserves some notice from the Catholic chaplain to the Mullingar gaol, as in that letter, the young baronet takes a bigoted fling at Catholic morality.*

All Ireland, at present, mourns over the sad and appalling fate of Brian Seery, who solemnly declared before his God that he had neither act, hand, part or knowledge in the crime for which he was to be hanged.

His innocence is believed and proclaimed by the people and by the press. Subscriptions pour in from England and from every part of Ireland, for the support of his afflicted widow and his five little orphans.

The man who actually attempted the assassination of Sir Francis Hopkins, tormented by his own conscience and in a fruitless desperation, openly declares that Brian Seery is innocent and that he himself is the man who fired at Sir Francis Hopkins. There is no secret in this affair – the man is known to the magistrates in the neighbourhood and to the police.

Under such circumstances, it might be expected that the prosecutor (Hopkins) would pause, reflect, and say, "Many mistakes have occurred in the identification of assailants. I was attacked in the darkness of night. The rattling of slugs were ringing in my ears. I was excited and, perhaps I was mistaken in swearing against Seery."

Such would be the thoughts of a diffident and humane Christian but, Sir Francis, in his own conceit, is infallible. He is vexed at the sympathy for Seery, as an innocent man and a martyr and, not satisfied with the result of his swearing at the commission, he rushes into print and attempts to fasten the infamous stain of perjury on the memory of the man who was sent by his testimony to a premature grave.

Brian Seery, on the scaffold, solemnly called God to witness the truth of his declaration of his innocence. Sir Francis, in his letter to the Freeman's Journal, *says that, "notwithstanding the reported dying declaration of innocence by Seery on the scaffold, I again affirm that he was the person that fired at me."*

It was better for the prosecutor to allow the ashes of Seery to sleep quiet in the grave than, in such a spirit of bitterness, come out with his angry assertion that Seery was not only a murderer during his life but, a perjurer in his dying breath. The public will easily decide whether they shall believe the last solemn declaration of a pious Catholic on the scaffold or, the angry affirmation of the prosecutor of the Sackville Street Club.

Sir Francis is annoyed at the comments that have been made by the press on the contradiction between the testimony of Mr French, the stipendiary magistrate and his own.

He tells us that he has letters from a policeman and an attorney's clerk to prove that he himself was right and then, in triumph, he concludes by saying, "the public can now fairly judge between Mr French's testimony and my own."

How a drowning man clutches at reeds; I wish the baronet may attempt an explanation in his next letter, of the contradiction between Sir Francis Hopkins on the first trial and Sir Francis Hopkins on the second. Will the police, or the attorney's clerk, stand to him on this point?

Report states that Mr French is to be sent out of the county for his swearing on the trial of Brian Seery and, why it was that the prosecutor volunteers an explanation on the contradiction with Mr French more than his contradiction with the other witnesses.

I am not able to tell but, this I can say with truth: if the Tories send Mr French out of the county, he will bring with him the blessings of the poor and the good wishes of every man who loves justice and the impartial administration of the law while, if Sir Francis Hopkins sells Rochfort and goes to the continent, as it is reported, his loss will not be felt, either as a guardian or a landlord and, his poor workmen can then hear mass on the holidays of the Catholic church.

I have the honour to be, dear Sir,

Your humble servant

J. Savage

Chapel House

Mullingar

~

Westmeath Guardian, Thursday, 5 March 1846

As a result of the international condemnation of Hopkins' evidence and indeed, the evidence of his close friends, the *Guardian* decided to come to the defence of this gang of assassins. This newspaper published, as they saw it, the strong evidence that "rightly" convicted Seery.

The strong Crown evidence that emerged during the trials was as follows:

1. Sir Francis Hopkins recognised Brian Seery during the struggle.
2. A hat was afterwards found at the scene and two policemen swore to having seen Seery wear the hat more than four months prior to the alleged attack.

~

That was it and, according to the Crown, Seery was justifiably convicted and executed on this evidence and, the fact that they deemed the defence of an alibi was not credible. However, on this occasion, the newspaper omitted to mention the coat or pipe and, the fact that these items were not mentioned in either of Hopkins' statements.

Let's take another look at this "concrete" evidence:

1. We have Hopkins returning from a party, full of wine or some other mind-altering substance. He alleges that someone fired a shot at him at very close range and missed, despite the fact that the gun discharged 18 slugs/bullets. He said the shooter ran and he ran after him. Hopkins was definitely handicapped – the result of partying and also, the steps he had to descend – yet, he managed to overtake the gunman at less than 35 yards. A struggle ensued and, as a result of this, he recognised Seery. According to Hopkins' evidence, not one of the servants in his house, at the time, heard the doorbell, the gunshot or the racket caused by the horse and the coachman shouting in order to control the horse. We know they would be listening out for him to return home. When a crime is committed, the police always look for a motive and, in this case, there was a motive, albeit in reverse. However, when they realised the reason that Hopkins mentioned Seery's name, they gave the "Bad Bart" their blessing and assisted him instigate proceedings, which ended in the murder of an innocent man. Seery had no motive to kill Hopkins, while he had a reason to keep him alive. However, Hopkins had a financial motive to eliminate Seery.

2. The famous hat. The *Guardian* said the hat was "afterwards" found. First of all, the crown witness who allegedly found the hat said, "I found the hat and my master a little after the shot was fired."
The above report, published three weeks after the execution of Seery, wasn't exactly spot on about the finding of the hat. According to the Prosecution, Thomas Telling, one of Hopkins' servants, said that he found the hat and gave it to Matthew Rogers. Rogers contradicted this and said Telling "showed him the hat." Hopkins said, "the hat was given to him by Thomas Telling the following morning" despite the fact that he was standing beside this famous hat when Telling picked it up. Wasn't it only natural for Mr Telling to hand it over to Hopkins then and there?

The report mentioned "the two policemen that swore to have seen Seery wear the hat some months prior to the alleged attack." That's true but, when their evidence is scrutinised, it becomes clear that they last saw Seery wear the hat more than four months prior to the alleged attack on Hopkins.

The four-month period (the policemen were estimating this time period), coincides with evidence from defence witness, Patrick Donohue. Donohue produced Seery's old hat in court and said Seery left it at his house in May. That's the reason that the policemen didn't see it for months. Constable Johnston also said that, during that period, he saw Seery wear a "Jerry Hat" (describing it as a hard-felt hat) and he did not wear the hat produced in court at that time. Johnson added, "I cannot say that the present band was on it in summer last or what band was on it then."

It is evident that Brian Seery was never the owner of the hat produced by the Prosecution in court. It's equally clear that the hat produced by the Defence was his hat. Seery hadn't laid eyes on it since May, never mind wear it. In my opinion, Constables Johnston and Doherty's evidence actually prove that Seery didn't wear the hat since the beginning of summer.

3. The *Guardian* failed to mention either the coat or the pipe. The pipe got very little mention in either of the trials, simply because Seery didn't smoke a pipe. According to the Prosecution, the coat was a very important piece of evidence. Let's take a look at how and when it arrived at Rochfort House.

Mrs Kiernan swore that it was taken from her home by the police, after the arrest of Seery and I believe her for the reasons that I will now outline.

Matthew Rogers, Steward to Hopkins stated that he found the coat at 7 o'clock that morning and handed it over to Mr Bookey (Sub-Inspector of Police).

Hopkins said, "Constable Johnston was first to show me the coat. This was at 5pm the following day."

It beggars belief that the coat was kept at the crime scene for more than 30 hours and, the senior police officer handed it over to a junior officer on his arrival at Rochfort House. It doesn't take a Sherlock Holmes to figure it out. Johnston was the policeman who removed the coat from Kiernan's house. Mrs Kiernan said that police took Seery's coat from her house on Thursday morning. Hopkins admitted that he didn't see the coat until Thursday evening, at 5pm so, that ties in with Mrs Kiernan's evidence.

Another thing that bothers me is that the Prosecution alleged that Seery removed his overcoat in the middle of a winter's night and left it down neatly at the 'crime scene'. He would not have removed clothing. It is very cold at the shore of the lake in the winter, especially at midnight. He wouldn't know if Hopkins was in the house, or out partying, or whatever. He could be there for hours, shivering in the cold as he waited for Hopkins to arrive home. An assassin moves into the killing zone. He shoots his victim and gets out as quickly as possible. He doesn't hang around to gather up his belongings. The above, together with everything mentioned in previous chapters, were ignored by the Prosecution and the *Westmeath Guardian* newspaper.

~

The editor added:

The public must decide between the external testimony of the witnesses and the internal evidence of the circumstances rather to be trusted, or the bare denial of the convict himself, standing at the foot of the gibbet, with sympathising thousands around him (at that time the only people around him were policemen and soldiers). *But the reliance to be placed on a last dying speech can only be estimated by experience and will be best understood by consulting the Newgate Calendar. We have no desire to contemplate human nature in her most monstrous shape, to reckon up the number of those who have perished with a lie upon their lips. The truth is, whatever maybe said to the contrary, the murder* (should be attempted murder) *was proved fairly and substantially and, much more satisfactorily (we appeal to those who have the largest of experience in criminal jurisprudence) than many cases where the convict has suffered the full penalty of the law and no one has dreamed of outrage.*

The law, therefore, whilst it refuses to listen to the declarations of a convict, where they intend to inculpate others without exculpating himself, would hardly be inclined to heed where their express object is to shuffle off the guilt from the convict himself (Seery never blamed or attempted to blame anyone else). Nor would it place reliance on his protestations of innocence made upon the scaffold. But Ireland it seems, rejecting these suggestions of experience and repudiating the lessons of the past, sympathises with the executed convict and believes him innocent. We know, for history teaches it too plainly, that in Ireland, the feeling of the people is never with the law but, always against it. Their sympathy is never with the innocent murdered but always, with the guilty murderer. We have yet to learn that such foolish displays of whining sentimentalism are any proof of innocence in their object. We have yet to be convinced that they prove anything more that the most pitiable folly on one hand and, the most perverse ignorance on the other.

~

The Sun, 21 March 1846

The case of Brian Seery, the man who was recently executed at Mullingar for shooting at Sir Francis Hopkins, has excited much painful interest and the discussion of which, like everything in Ireland, has been disfigured by politics and polemics. Seery, a Roman Catholic, died with a strong protestation of his innocence. The clergyman who attended him in his last moments, declares that Seery was a murdered man and that the real culprit is at large and known, and Sir Francis Hopkins has been fiercely assailed for some alleged discrepancies between his original statement and his evidence at the trial. Seery had been acquitted by one jury (actually it was a hung jury, ten for a guilty verdict and two against) *but, was indicted again and convicted by another jury – tried twice for the same offence, a circumstance almost unprecedented in the history of criminal jurisprudence to many. The country people, to mark their appreciation of his innocence, kept within doors on the day of the execution and spectators of a dying man's struggles, in a populous neighbourhood, consisted exclusively of the soldiers and the police. Irrespective of the guilt or innocence of the man, the moral effect of the punishment is perfectly worthless while such an impression prevails. The Irish journals have been discussing the subject with intense fever and it has been taken up by the London journals in a spirit hardly less energetic. Subscriptions are being raised for the widow and children of Seery who, are likely to fare well by the sympathy thus created in their favour.*

~

Snippets Taken from *The Tablet* Report, 28 February 1846

If the facts be truly reported and really, there seems to be no difference of opinion on this point, we have no hesitation in saying that, if it be murder to employ against a man, an instrument or means which are sure to bring about his death, whether he be innocent or guilty, then Brian Seery is a murdered man.

~

It was decided to put Seery on trial a second time. On this occasion, the British ensured that there should be no half-measures taken. They were determined that he should be brought before a bigoted, tried and trusted, partisan, hanging jury. Three Catholic members of the Grand Jury Panel were challenged on the part of the Prosecution. The British rejected any notion to have Brian Seery tried by any, other than blood-thirsty, anti-Irish members of the gentry. The gentlemen who were challenged and rejected from the jury, were rejected from the jury solely on the ground of them being Catholic. The British came up with numerous excuses but, let's call a spade a spade, as far as the British were concerned, Seery had to die. He had to be made a sacrifice of in order to satisfy the demands of a mob of blood-thirsty loyalist landlords.

~

The Tablet again

We declare to God, we would just as soon be tried for our lives before a mob of lynchers in the Far West, as before one of these loyalist Juries, bounded on by Crown advisers so utterly lost to all sense of decency, as were those who conducted the case of Brian Seery.

~

The Tablet Quotes the *Evening Mail* of 16 February 1846:

We understand that there is now evidence to show that the alibi, in all its minute details, was got up and arranged before the crime was committed and that the Attorney General, as moderate as well as merciful a man as lives, is in possession of the particulars. We repeat that which we stated on a former occasion: that in our opinion, the Attorney General was exercising a sound discretion in setting aside Roman Catholics on the jury. He and the Government, we understand, repudiate any such distinction – the fact being admitted, and we are sorry for it. The bold and manly course would be directly the reverse. A conspiracy is raging in Ireland, possessing all the characteristics of a civil war of population against property, of creed against religion. It is a war of Papists against Protestants, the confederates or conspirators being exclusively Roman Catholics and bound by a terrible oath to exterminate, even by death, the professors of the creed opposed to them. This is the Ribbon obligation, described and denounced by Lord Plunkett. We repeat that no Roman Catholic should sit on a jury.

~

No such evidence existed to prove that an alibi, in all its minute details, was set up before the commission of the crime. However, the British Government used it in an attempt to get out of the predicament they found themselves in after the murder of Seery.

~

More from *The Tablet*

We are afraid our readers will think we are joking with them, when we state what that secret evidence is what in Ireland passes current for taking away men's lives upon the gallows.

~

Back to the *Evening Mail*

There were two men concerned in this outrage. One of these, with whom Sir Francis grappled, fell over a low paling and must have cut his shins and otherwise injured himself. A man had been seen walking with Seery a day previous to the outrage and, upon that man being taken up and examined a day after, he had his shins cut. Upon comparing the height of the cuts in the shins with the paling, there was an exact correspondence. Therefore, there was no doubt, the man with the broken shins must have been at the outrage. Therefore, Seery, who was seen with him the day before, must have accompanied him to the outrage. Therefore, Seery must have been guilty.

~

I, just like *The Tablet*, have a massive problem with this so called "strong evidence". A man, seen with Seery the day before the alleged attack, had scrapes or cuts on his shins (this as the British saw it), was strong enough evidence to justify the murder of Brian Seery. It also begs the question, why wasn't this man charged, convicted and murdered, just like Seery?

Hopkins himself stated that the man he grappled with ran and fell as he was running; he said nothing about falling over a low paling. The fact is, if a man was running and fell over a low paling, he wouldn't damage both shins at the same height as the paling. While running, there would only be only one foot on the ground at any given time. Another problem with this evidence is, as Hopkins swore that the man he was grappling with was Seery and Seery was the man, he said, fell after the tussle, how would the cuts and scrapes transfer to the other man's shins. Hopkins said all along that it was Seery who fell; he never mentioned the other man falling. What he did say about the second man was, "I dealt him a severe blow with my left hand and knocked him down."

The coachman, William Pallinger said, he saw one man fall and this was before the shot was fired. However, according to Hopkins, the man fell after the shot was fired. Seemingly, this story has brought to life by another Hollywood character, "The invisible Man". What has this cock-and-bull story got to do with discrediting the evidence of decent, honest, respectable people? Absolutely nothing. Pallinger, just like Hopkins, mentioned nothing about anyone falling over a low paling.

This so-called "strong secret evidence" wasn't used during the trials simply because, it was only concocted afterwards, in an attempt to counter unfavourable national and international media reports. The British realised that they had been found out and decided to continue doing what they always did – make it up as they went along. The British regime was the ISIS terror group of 19th century Ireland: murder came natural to them. However, there is a big difference between these two terror groups: The British did their utmost to sweep everything under the carpet. The same British terrorists, in one week in 1827, murdered 12 captives in my hometown of Mullingar. On the other hand, ISIS sweep nothing under the carpet. They let the world know that they are, just like the British were, capable of carrying out atrocities at the drop of a hat.

~

The Letters

Father Savage's letter really hit the nail on the head. Hopkin's went to pieces as a result of this letter. National and international response to his ever-changing evidence didn't help either. Hopkins letter stated that Mr French admitted, on the 1st December last, to having heard Seery's name mentioned. He went on to say that Mr French gave his reasons to Mr Seed (the Crown Solicitor) for not inserting it in the first information. Hopkins claimed it was said, in the presence of Mr Browne, his clerk, Mr Bookey, Sub Inspector of Constabulary in Mullingar, Hopkins himself and others. However, Hopkins declined to call his friends as witnesses to support his case with sworn evidence.

The most worrying correspondence in the above-mentioned letters, in my opinion, was written by the Crown Solicitor, Mr S. Seed and mailed to Richard Pennefather, Dublin Castle (second last paragraph of first letter – see *Chapter 6*). This man, in an attempt to secure a conviction, admitted he approached "many members of the Grand Jury" prior to the commencement of Seery's second trial.

They got their conviction and execution but, the execution didn't turn out as the British had hoped. They used executions to put the frighteners on the locals and indeed, on people all over these islands and further afield. However, the Church snookered their plans and asked the parishioners to keep indoors at the time of the execution. The only people in attendance, and there were a large number of them, were members of the army and police force.

Hopkins had great difficulty coming to terms with the role he played in the murder of Brian Seery. The repercussions he suffered at the hands of the locals didn't help either. It became too dangerous for him to remain in the Mullingar area. He didn't feel safe and decided to leave the country. Alice Nolan in her book, *The Byrne's of Glengoulah*, gave an account of Seery's trial. Her account was taken verbatim from the *Dublin Nation* newspaper of January and February 1846. She states the following:

> *It's a well-established fact that, after the execution of Brian Seery, Sir Francis Hopkins is obliged to be strapped to a bed at the Club House, Sackville Street (O'Connell Street).*

Alice later discovered that Hopkins died, a lunatic, on the continent.

Any right-thinking person would come to the conclusion that this evil man was riddled with guilt, knowing full well that he and his cronies (primarily him), were responsible for the legal murder of Brian Seery. He suffered nightmares brought about by his greed: Hopkins just didn't want to honour his agreement with Seery. After all, to people like him, money is their God. Paying a year's rent for Seery's new farm would be deemed, by people of Hopkins stamp to be a mortal sin. We all know that in the world of the gentry, "money is money".

Father Savage mentioned the man who confessed to the crime after Seery was convicted and sentenced to death. He stated that, the man's reason for not coming forward prior to the trial was because, he believed Seery could not be convicted on the flimsy evidence produced by the Prosecution. This man was taken into custody, his head shaved and was placed in a lunatic asylum. In all honesty the British couldn't pardon Seery and charge this man because, in doing so, they would also have to charge Hopkins with the crime of perjury.

The unnamed man's confession warranted another look at the alleged attack on Hopkins. Maybe he is responsible – that is, if an attack took place at all. However, I'm very reluctant to believe this unfortunate man was the culprit. This sort of behaviour is still in vogue in today's world. He wasn't the first, or last man to approach the police and confess to a serious crime. I actually knew a local Mullingar man who, in the 1960s, walked into a Garda station and confessed to a murder he couldn't possibly be responsible for. Years later, the real killer was charged and jailed for life thanks to his DNA matching the crime scene evidence.

A large number of very respectable witnesses put Seery about eight miles from the scene of the crime and that evidence alone warranted a dismissal of the proceedings. The alleged finding and linking of the coat and hat was a blatant lie. The Crown Solicitor's letter to Dublin Castle, verifying the fact that he briefed Grand Jury members prior to the second trial was a disgrace. So, what really happened, Sir Francis Hopkins stated that he attended a party on the night in question. He admitted he spent about five hours in the company of Col Caulfield and friends, partying. Of course, the best and most expensive wine was flowing and free. It's not unreasonable to believe that Hopkins returned home in a drunken state. He admitted that he opened the carriage door himself and stepped out, unaided by the coachman (of course, it's possible that he fell out). This behaviour was very unusual. The gentry always waited on the coachman to open the door. If Hopkins didn't fall out of the carriage, he definitely fell as he was climbing the steps leading to the hall door, banging his head a few times as he fell down the steps. Hopkins, a magistrate, felt he couldn't turn up in court appearing like a drunk nursing a hangover. I'm sure he looked like some of the unfortunates who appeared before him on a regular basis and he couldn't afford to be seen like that. He devised a plan to justify his battered appearance and, at the same time, nullify his rent agreement with Brian Seery. I say this, as I don't believe there is man that ever lived who could have missed a full-grown adult at the stated distance between him and the alleged gunman, especially when using a blunderbuss as his weapon of choice.

~

Quotes and Opinions

A month after the alleged attack, Lord Castlemaine, while addressing a meeting of the magistrates of County Westmeath held at Dublin Castle said:

> *We, the magistrates of the County Westmeath, cannot allow this meeting to separate without offering our sincere and heartfelt*

congratulations to Sir Francis Hopkins on his late providential escape and, of recording our admiration of his cool, manly and determined conduct under such sudden and desperate circumstances.

These same men met, at the Hopkins residence, the day after the alleged attack and gladly took their instructions from Hopkins. Despite contradictions in his story, they believed everything he said and pledged allegiance to this evil man. It was also a month before some of these magistrates would sit, with other members of the gentry, on a packed jury and dish out a guilty verdict, leading to a death sentence being imposed and carried out on the unfortunate Seery, an innocent Irishman.

~

Charles Dickens Letter to the *Daily News*, 23 February 1846

Dickens always had a problem with capital punishment however, it wasn't until after the execution of Brian Seery that he put pen to paper. He mailed a letter to the *Daily News* that was published on 23 February 1846. An account of it is outlined below. He asked and answered the following two questions:

Whether the death penalty encouraged repentance and reform and whether fallible human beings were justified in imposing such an irrevocable punishment? In reply to the first question, Dickens argues that the interval between the sentence and execution is far too short and stressful to allow serious contemplation, whatever religious believers and idealists like to believe. His response to the second question is equally firm. Citing the recent case of the Irishman, Brian Seery, who had been executed for attempting to kill his former landlord despite extremely questionable evidence and his own persistent protestations of innocence, Dickens declares:
The barest possibility of mistake is sufficient reason against the taking of a life, which nothing can restore.*

~

---

* *Letters from Charles Dickens on capital punishment, 23 February - 16 March 1846.* British Library website (https://www.bl.uk/collection-items/letters-from-charles-dickens-on-capital-punishment-23-february---16-march-1846)

House of Commons Report 23 February 1846

Daniel O'Connell put the following questions to the Right Hon. Baronet, the Secretary for the Home Department, Sir J. Graham:

1st Question: Whether a deputation consisting of several persons waited on His Excellency, the Lord Lieutenant, after the conviction and before the execution of Brian Seery, to pray that the convict should not be respited or, his sentence transmuted but, that he should be executed?

2nd Question: To ask whether there be any instance in England, for the last century, of any person being tried for any capital felony by a second jury, after the first jury was discharged by the court at the same session of assizes and convicted and executed? If so, state the time, place and name of the individual?

Sir Graham's reply to the first question:

I have to inform the Hon. Gentleman that a deputation from the County of Westmeath did wait upon the Lord Lieutenant before the execution of Seery and made upon their own part that the law should be allowed take its course. I deeply regret the interference in this harsh and unusual manner. I must, however, be permitted to observe that the interference had no effect whatever upon the decision of His Excellency, that decision having been come to exclusively upon the most careful consideration of the notes of the evidence and of the opinion of the jury and the judge who tried the case.

Sir Graham's reply to the second question:

I am not so versed or practiced in the law as to be able to give him direct authorities on the subject however, I think I may say this, that it is an old principle of law, recognised throughout the United Kingdom, that a party accused of a felony may be put upon his trial upon an indictment until he be acquitted or convicted by a jury of his country. That is undoubtedly the law. The hon. and learned Gentleman asks, what cases have occurred in England of persons being tried for a capital felony by a second jury after the first jury was discharged. I will answer the question.
In 1794, at the summer assizes of York, before Mr Justice Lawrence, a person charged with murder was convicted and executed, the judge having discharged the first jury and ordered a second to be sworn, by which he was found guilty. I should not be dealing candidly with the House if I did not state, there is a distinction in this case: the judge had not summed up and a juror had taken ill. Mr Justice Lawrence,

having referred to the notes of Mr Justice Buller in a like case, decided that the first jury should be discharged, a second jury empanelled and, the trial should proceed.

It may be said that, in the present case, the opinion of the jury was formed and expressed in open court.

The House will allow me to say that in a recent case, on the Midland Circuit, the identical point was decided. At the last spring assizes, a female of the name of Hannah Jarvis was indicted before Mr Justice Coltman, the jury could come to no decision and their difference of opinion continuing at the close of the assizes, they were discharged by the learned judge. In the summer assizes the prisoner was again brought up on the same indictment, before Mr Justice Maule. A second jury was empanelled and, they proceeded to trial, which ended in acquittal but, the principle was the same.

With regard to the law and practice in such matters, they were both ruled, in this case, by two of the ablest criminal judges of Ireland – the Chief Justice of the Common Pleas, and the Chief Baron of the Exchequer. Before proceeding to the second trail, the points were solemnly argued and the judgement was pronounced by Chief Baron Brady, who also pronounced the sentence. The Lord Lieutenant acted upon the opinions of these learned judges in directing that the prisoner should undergo the extreme penalty of the law.

Daniel O'Connell alluded to a case in which he had been counsel, when Chief Justice Pennefather ruled that his (O'Connell's) argument was inconsistent with the practice and the trial was proceeded with. The twelve judges met on the subject and, though they gave no decision, it was understood that they had formed an opinion adverse to that of Chief Justice Pennefather.[*]

While allowing the second Seery trial to proceed, Chief Justice Doherty cited the same case and stated as follows,

A course very similar to the present, having been proposed to be taken at the Special Commission which occurred in Cork in the year 1829. The learned judge who presided, submitted to the twelve judges two questions: first, whether a jury discharged under circumstances resembling what had occurred on the present occasion, namely, the illness of a juror and the risk to his life which he would run if he were longer confined, the judges unanimously pronounced upon the legality

---

[*] Pennefather was known throughout the UK as the "Vicious Tory". See, for example, *A consideration of the state of Ireland in the nineteenth century* by G. Locker Lampson (A. Constable, London, 1907).

of that course. Second, whether a prisoner so situated could be put upon his trial on the following morning and to this question also, the judges gave an affirmative decision, thus declaring that both courses were perfectly legal.

Doherty added:

... under all the circumstances, the court could not grant the application.

Daniel O'Connell, an honest man, stated that the twelve judges gave no decision. O'Connell should know, he was at court in Cork on the day in question and he represented the defendant. In my opinion, Chief Justice Doherty lied in order to justify his decision to proceed with the second trial.

Dealing with Graham's response to the first question, and the admission that a deputation from Westmeath lobbied the Lord Lieutenant, requesting that the law should take its course, who were these guys? Did any of them sit on either jury? Did any of them call to see Hopkins the day after the alleged attack? Were they magistrates? Who were they? Their names, to my knowledge were never published, no minutes were taken, no record of the meeting exists. Daniel O'Connell learned of this despicable deed from a letter written by Most Rev Dr Cantwell, the Catholic Bishop of Meath.

In Graham's response to the second question, he is not comparing like with like. In the first example, the 1794 murder trial before Mr Justice Lawrence, Graham fully accepts that the jury was dismissed before the completion of the trial. During the 1794, trial a juror had taken ill, at this stage the opinion of the jury was not formed one way or the other and the judge hadn't an opportunity to sum up. Despite being asked, Graham failed to name the defendant. Seemingly, this man was making it up as he went along.

The second example, a more recent case involving a lady named Hannah Jarvis. In the 1845 spring assizes, she was indicted before Mr Justice Coltman. The jury, in her case, were discharged as they could not agree. In the summer assizes, she was again brought up on the same indictment before a different judge, Mr Justice Maule. A second jury was empanelled and they proceeded to trial. Besides being tried by a different judge, the other differences in this lady's case and Seery's case were: her trial was postponed from spring until summer; she had an extra three months to prepare her defence. Seery met his defence team for the first time a few days prior to the commencement of the initial trial. Seery's defence team were also appointed to represent all the defendants appearing at the Commission that week so, it's not surprising that they required more time to study the evidence. The defence team, quite rightly, pleaded with the court to postpone Seery's second trial until the next assizes.

The Crown Attorney replied that if the object of the learned council was merely to postpone the case to the following morning, he would not oppose the application but, if a longer postponement were required, he would object to it. The Crown's objection was successful and, the second trial began the next day, before the same judge. We now know Seery was convicted and executed for the attempted murder of the "goose that was about to lay the golden egg", which, of course, is ridiculous.

Chapter 8

Investigation into Conduct of Arthur French

Shortly after Seery's execution Hopkins creditability went from bad to worse. He really believed that his situation could not possibly worsen but, it did. He pestered people in authority for their assistance in an attempt to alleviate the difficulties he was experiencing. He persuaded a number of people to write letters of support to his claim that he did mention Seery's name while giving his first statement to Mr French. His friends in turn lobbied their contacts at Dublin Castle and the Houses of Parliament in London. (A number of these letters later appeared in the *Westmeath Guardian* on 14 May 1846).

Hopkins appealed to members of the gentry to state that they heard him mention Seery's name to Mr French. However, there were only five people in the room when Hopkins made the first statement and, after listening to Mr French read aloud the contents, two of these gentlemen – magistrates, John Lyons and William Reilly – certified the content of the statement as a true and accurate recording of the evidence given to Mr French by Hopkins. However, a number of weeks later, Lyons tried to backtrack, in an attempt to help his friend out of the predicament. The third person present was of course, Hopkins and after listening to Mr French read the statement, he decided to read it himself. After doing so, he immediately certified everything as correct and right by signing on the dotted line. The fourth person, Dr Ferguson, said that Hopkins mentioned Seery's name to him during a conversation, he did not say that he heard Hopkins mention the name to Mr French. The fifth person was Mr French and we know what he had to say about Hopkins version of events.

Having taken all this on board, the "Bad Bart" realised he had a lot of work to do, he wrote to a number of friends, asking them to state that they were in his house on 1st December, which was two weeks after the alleged attack. Some wrote back, stating they were not present at the time in question (of course, he knew they weren't). Some of the remainder stated they were present and witnessed French admit that he heard Hopkins mention Seery's name, adding, he also gave his reason as to why the name was omitted from the informations. However, they gave contradictory evidence – even contradicting some of the sworn evidence Hopkins gave during the first trial.

Hopkins, in turn, wrote a letter of complaint to Sir James Graham, Houses of Parliament, London (this was the man who was questioned by Daniel O'Connell about Seery's execution). Eventually, the Government reluctantly agreed to act under the Laws relating to the Constabulary of Ireland. Mr Henry Baldwin, Q.C. was appointed to hold a

Court of Inquiry at Dublin Castle, on Monday, the 11th day of May 1846 and the following days, in order to investigate all such matters as shall, then and there, be brought before them affecting the conduct of Mr Arthur French.

Mr Baldwin, a magistrate, was appointed under and by virtue of the recited Act and to examine, on oath, into the truth of such charges as may be preferred against such magistrate and to report onto the Government accordingly."

On the appointed day, the investigation began by calling on Sir Francis Hopkins to read his statement. Hopkins stated:

The plainest statement I can make is to refer to the letter I addressed to the Right Hon. Baronet, the Secretary for the Home Department, Sir James Graham, which was as follows:

Sir,

I have the honour to forward for your information, the enclosed correspondence, the originals of which are in my possession and ready, if necessary, for your inspection. By it, I would call your attention to the conduct of Mr French, stipendiary magistrate stationed at Mullingar in the county of Westmeath, who, on the trial of Brian Seery, gave such evidence as renders inquiry imperatively necessary. Previous to the committal of Brian Seery, two informations were taken on the same day by Mr French. The first, at eleven o'clock am, the second at five o'clock pm. In the first information, the name of Seery was omitted; in the second information, it was inserted. I stated, on oath, on the trial that I had mentioned the name of Seery at the time the first information was taken. Mr French, the stipendiary magistrate who took these informations, swore that I had not mentioned any name. Aware of the very injurious effects that have already been produced, as regards the due administration of justice in Ireland by those strange and unaccountable discrepancies, I deem it a duty, which I owe, not only to myself but to the country, to take the step I now do and I rest confident that in your hands, the case will meet with that full consideration which its importance deserves.
I may be permitted to observe that daily expecting that some investigating would have been made touching this matter, I have

*hitherto abstained from calling your attention to it but, finding Mr
French continues in office without adequate inquiry having been made.
I am led to suppose that by some oversight, it has been permitted to
pass unnoticed by the authorities.*

Hopkins continued:

*The informations were sworn in my bedroom. It was written down by
Mr French who was at a table close to me. There were a lot of
gentlemen downstairs. While downstairs, they were discussing the
attack. The name of Brian Seery was mentioned on several occasions.
Mr French was present and, I believe, in his hearing. While downstairs
I repeated the substance of the attack to Mr French and again
mentioned the name of Brian Seery.*
*While taking the first information in my bedroom, Mr French did not
take it from my dictation, I mentioned it in a general way.*
*When the information was drawn up, Mr French asked me if it was a
true recording. He read it aloud. I did not notice the absence of Brian
Seery's name. There were about five gentlemen present: Mr French,
myself, Mr William Reilly, Mr John Lyons and Dr Ferguson. Reilly
and Lyons were the magistrates who signed the informations. While
they were drawing up, I was engaged in conservation. There was a
good deal of conversation at the time.*

In reply to a question, whether Mr French might have heard the name,
Hopkins replied:

*If busy occupied writing, I could not say what another heard. Brian
Seery's name was mentioned by me upstairs in the bedroom. I used
Seery's name before numerous times in the library. Gentlemen
continued to come in from time to time to the library. The only charge I
make against Mr French is stating that I did not give the name in the
first information and the charge that he was previously aware that
Brian Seery was to shoot at me.*

Cross-examined by Mr Bessonet Q.C. for Mr French, Hopkins said:

*I spoke about the trial of Brian Seery in Mr French's presence. He was
present with the other magistrates. I spoke in my usual tone of voice. I
read the information before signing them.*

To the Court:

*Mr French read them for me and I read them myself. I did not make
any observation that the name of Brian Seery was omitted. Previous to*

November last, Mr French notified me that there was some intelligence indicating the possibility of an attack being carried out against me. Prior to that, I had been informed by others. I was not told that John Morton or Brian Seery was to do me injury.

To Mr French:

I do not recall any information, on any prior occasion, given to me by you.

To the Court:

The second statement was sworn at about five o'clock in the afternoon. It was taken in the hall.

Hopkins then said:

I signed it in the library, not the hall and numerous persons were present, Seery, and several others. Seery was then arrested and taken into custody and I, at once, identified him. Immediately after the identification, the second statement was taken. I have no idea if Mr Reilly stated on oath that Brian Seery was not involved.

To the Court:

It is my positive impression that Mr French heard me mention Brian Seery previous to drawing up the first information. I am positive that I mentioned the name of Brian Seery.
At Rochfort on 1st December, I heard Mr French confirm that he heard the name of Brian Seery mentioned prior to the first information being taken, and he stated his reason for not putting it into the statement. The reason he gave was "I did it for the best". The Crown Solicitor, Mr Seed, his clerk and many others were present.

To the Court:

I particularly named Seery on the first occasion. I have no doubt about that whatsoever.

The Court:

Was Seery a tall man?

Hopkins:

Rather tall.

The Court:

> *The information goes on, "... and deponent (Hopkins) said, there is one of the men, whom he would know on seeing again." Who was that?*

Hopkins:

> *Brian Seery*

The Court:

> *Did you observe that statement in the information before you swore it – because that would imply that the man was not known?*

Hopkins:

> *I did not remark it. This is all I have to state with reference to the first charge!*

~

From my notes:

Among the letters referred to, one was from Mr Lyons, another from Mr Reilly. These are the two magistrates who were present when Hopkins gave his first statement. There were also letters from Mr Seed, Mr Vignoles, Mr Browne and Dr Ferguson. In these letters, some of the authors stated that Mr French informed them, with respect to the omission of the name, "that he did it for the best." It appeared, from the several letters that the writers considered, that Mr French admitted the omission to have been entirely his own, not anything on the part of Sir Francis Hopkins.

~

Back to the investigation:

Mr Baldwin inquired if any of the gentlemen who wrote the letters were in town. If possible, it would be most desirable to have some of them examined.

Mr French stated:

> *The question for the court is the amount of accuracy with regard to the mention of Brian Seery's name in the bedroom.*

Mr Baldwin:

> *If you choose to object to the letters, you are legally at liberty to do so.*

Mr Bessonet and Mr French both said that they did not impugn, in the least, the writers of the letters.

Mr Bessonet, for the Defence, said:

> *Sir Francis merely stated what he believed to be true. Mr French has*
> *two things to do to satisfy you and, I hope, Sir Francis Hopkins, about*
> *an isolated fact. Also, the government and Sir Francis Hopkins as to*
> *his conduct as a magistrate employed by the government. With*
> *reference to the second charge, I think there will be little or no trouble*
> *about that. No one can suppose Mr French did not intend to do his*
> *duty, in every respect, towards the government, Sir Francis Hopkins*
> *and himself.*
> *On the morning of the 19th of November, on learning of the attack on*
> *Sir Francis Hopkins, Mr French rode to Rochfort in his role as the*
> *government magistrate of the county of Westmeath. He did not see Sir*
> *Francis when he first entered the house. Mr Bookey arrived shortly*
> *after and Mr French and Mr Bookey had a conversation in respect of*
> *the attack on Sir Francis. Mr Bookey informed Mr French that the*
> *police were searching for a man named Brian Seery, who Sir Francis*
> *suspected had fired at him.*

Mr Bessonet read a letter from Dr Ferguson. The letter contained information about the attack that was made and that Sir Francis Hopkins suspected Brian Seery. The letter describes Seery's personal appearance adding that there was no warrant issued authorising the police to search for Seery.

On reading the letter, Mr Bookey sent out police to look for him. This led Mr French to use great caution. He was then aware that Sir Francis Hopkins suspected Seery. Numerous gentlemen arrived and engaged in a conversation. Mr French is not denying that he heard the details of the incident being discussed however, it was a case of suspicion and it was Mr French's duty to be accordingly cautious. He considered it his duty to prefer a personal to a nominal identification and, nothing occurred to change his mind about this until about five o'clock in the afternoon, when Sir Francis pointed at Seery and said, "That's the man." Once Seery was identified, all doubt vanished from Mr French's mind.

Earlier that morning, Mr Lyons suggested to Sir Francis to go upstairs to the bedroom. He was followed by Mr French, Dr Ferguson, Mr Reilly and Mr Lyons. A conversation took place concerning the informations about to be taken.

> *Sir Francis said that he mentioned the name of Brian Seery, not to Mr*
> *French personally but, in the hearing of all the gentlemen in the room.*

Mr French read the information aloud. Sir Francis also read it and remarked that the assailant who attacked him first was a tall man and the other, a little smaller. Sir Francis added:

... he would know one of the men if he saw him again.

Mr Bessonet remarked, very ably, on the fact that no notice was observed by the omission of Seery's name, either by Hopkins, Lyons or Reilly – the magistrates present. After the information was taken, Mr French waited a considerable time to see if Seery would be taken.

When Seery arrived at Rochfort, Mr French wished to have the prisoner produced with others, for the purpose of having a general identification. He collected several countrymen and mixed Seery among them to form a line up. Immediately after Sir Francis Hopkins identified him, Mr French took the second information, issued his warrant and Seery was sent to gaol.

When Mr Seed arrived at Rochfort on 1st December, he asked Mr French if, at the time Sir Francis made the first information, he had mentioned the name of Brian Seery. Mr French said, no.

Mr Seed then asked if the other two magistrates were of the same opinion. Mr French said that he did not know.

Mr Seed then requested Mr French to ask them. Mr French did so and the answers were,

They did not think any name had been mentioned.

Mr Bessonet read a letter from Mr Reilly, corroborating this statement. On the second trial, at the Special Commission, Mr Lyons swore a name was mentioned. A letter was then read from Mr Lyons to the purport that, as Mr French was writing the information, a conversation took place between him (Mr Lyons) and Sir Francis Hopkins. It was probable that Mr French did not hear the name, and this accounts for the testimony he gave at the trial. Mr French then, having cause to suppose from the information he received, that it was a case only of suspicion and treated it as such.

Mr French was not examined on the first trial. At the second trial, the witnesses were kept out of court until called in for examination. Mr French was then asked,

At the time the first informations were taken, did Sir Francis mention any name to you?

He replied:

No.

Mr Lyons is quite consistent with that, – that Sir Francis had mentioned a name and Mr French had not heard it.

On cross-examination, Mr French was asked:

> *Was it possible that Sir Francis mentioned Seery's name and you not hear it?*

Mr French answered:

> *Very possibly he might,*

adding that he was ready to meet any inquiry.

The Attorney General replied that:

> *An inquiry will not be necessary.*

Mr Bessonet stated:

> *I adopt the letters that have been written by the gentlemen. Mr French was worried that justice would not be done and that, on a satisfactory identification, the man who had assaulted Sir F. Hopkins should be punished.*

After commenting on the letters and pointing out numerous discrepancies, Mr Bessonet replied that the facts showed, Mr French could not be considered as a magistrate not desirous of fulfilling his duty. Until the case is brought up to that, Mr French could not be convicted. It was of no benefit to Mr French to swear to what he did not believe to be true. The government believed there was nothing to inquire about.

Mr Bessonet continued:

> *The greatest anxiety was shown by Mr Lyons to explain the answer he gave at the trial but, this was not allowed. Here are two magistrates who say they heard no name mentioned at the time. Dr Ferguson, the medical gentleman says nothing on the subject* (i.e. of hearing Hopkins mention Seery's name to Mr French) *and Sir Francis is alone on the other side. The case is entirely on their testimony; I leave it with you on that branch of the case.*

Mr Bessonet again:

> *With respect to the second charge, Mr French received information three years ago that two men, Barney Seery* (not Brian) *and John Martin intended to injure Sir F. Hopkins. What did he do? He*

immediately informed Sir Francis Hopkins of it. About a year ago, he received similar information and he instantly communicated it.

Mr Bessonet continued by stating that he felt the greatest anxiety to satisfy Sir Francis Hopkins, that Mr French had no further or other desire than to do every justice. He was actuated by truth in his conduct and did not act otherwise than, from a feeling to protect Sir Francis Hopkins and, rested his case upon his honour and as a gentleman and his character as a Christian.

In reply to Hopkins, Mr French stated:

That he had not seen the letter from Dr Ferguson to Mr Bookey previous to taking the informations. He added that from that time until the period of identification he considered the case against Brian Seery as one of suspicion merely. He heard the name mentioned repeatedly in the library.

To the Court, Mr French stated:

I cannot remember hearing Sir Francis Hopkins mention the name of Brian Seery. It was mentioned by Bookey and others. I was the person who drew the informations. I got the general description from the groom and some others and, drew them up in the general way designedly – not wishing to pin Sir Francis to any description until a personal identification would take place. I read the informations aloud. I was not examined on the first trial; I was on the second. I then swore that, at the time of taking the first information, I did not hear the name of Brian Seery used by Sir Francis Hopkins. He might have mentioned the name and I not hear it. I said so at the trial.

Tuesday, 12 May 1846

Mr Seed, the Crown Solicitor stated:

On the 1st of December, I went to Sir Francis Hopkins house. I was accompanied by Mr Brennan. Mr French arrived shortly after. I had a conversation with Mr French in the library on the subject of the depositions. I informed him that I had come down, by direction of the Government, to inquire into the reason why Brian Seery's name had not been mentioned as to that case.
Mr French stated that he did not wish to put any name into the first informations, lest there might be two persons of the name of Brian Seery, or a person of the name of Patrick Seery and, that he thought that it might not be right to pin Sir Francis to any particular name until he identified the person who had attacked him.

I stated to him that, "it was a very important fact and one which it was desirable that should be satisfactorily explained."

I asked Sir Francis Hopkins if he had "mentioned the name to Mr French?"

Sir Francis said he had.

Mr Lyons, the magistrate, then came in and there was a conversation then with respect to the subject.

I asked Mr Lyons if the name of Brian Seery had been mentioned. He replied, "It had been mentioned by Sir Francis Hopkins."

I asked Mr French, at my office at Mullingar prior to the trial, if Sir Francis had mentioned the name before the first information was sworn.

I think he said, he had not. I think he said that, "Seery's name was mentioned by several persons who were present the morning the informations were taken but, I cannot charge my memory as to how it was mentioned."

I told Mr French that, it would be necessary for me to report to the government his reasons for not putting the name in the informations and I read over my report, which I have here and, it was approved by him.

Mr Seed asked Mr Baldwin if he was at liberty to read that report on the present inquiry.

Mr Baldwin replied:

Yes, certainly.

Mr Seed read his report. It contained the facts already before the public.

Sir Francis Hopkins asked Mr Seed:

Did you not hear Mr Lyons say that he heard me mention the name to Mr French and, did not Mr French acknowledge that he heard me mention the name?

Mr Seed replied:

I remember Mr Lyons stating that he heard you mention the name but, I do not remember Mr French stating it.

Mr French put some questions to Mr Seed. He answered as follows:

I think you said that either Mr Lyons or Reilly, or both, said that they agreed with you, that the name of Brian Seery was not mentioned by Sir Francis Hopkins on the first occasion. I am not positive that both said so. I recollect, I heard you say that Mr Reilly and Mr Lyons had agreed in your opinion.

Mr Seed then read a letter from Mr Lyons to Mr French, which stated that:

When the police come back, you must take a short information against Brian Seery as the person who committed the offence.

Mr Seed agreed that:

If informations founded upon a private conservation, held between two gentlemen, were sworn, it would be most improper. The clear impression, on my mind, is that Mr French knew the name of Brian Seery.

Sir Francis Hopkins:

Have you any doubt that, when Mr French assigned his reasons for the omission of Brian Seery's name, it had reference to the time at which the first information's were taken?

Mr Seed replied:

The reference, on my mind, is that the reasons he gave were tantamount to an acknowledgement that the name had been mentioned.

Sir Francis Hopkins:

And that he did not think it prudent to put the name into the first information?

Mr Seed:

Precisely so.

Mr French:

And you were quite right, there can be no doubt that I thought it more prudent.

Sir Francis Hopkins said that hitherto, the line of defence adopted was that the name had not been mentioned, at or before taking the first information. In consequence of that representation, comments had been made by the public press, which had strongly influenced the public mind. It now appears that Mr French acknowledged that he had repeatedly heard the name of Brian Seery, before the first information was taken. That was a most important admission and one which he (Sir Francis), hoped would obtain circulation, equally as extensive as the original representation or rather, original impression.

Mr Bessonet, for Mr French, said:

> *It was an admitted fact that Mr French had heard the name of Seery from Mr Bookey before the first information was lodged. That fact was undeniable and undenied but, what he did deny was that he heard it from Sir Francis Hopkins.*
> *At the trial of Seery in Mullingar, the question was distinctly put to Mr French, "Did Sir Francis, at the drawing up of the first information, mention any name to you?"*
> *Mr French's reply was emphatically, "No."*
> *Mr French was then asked, "If Sir Francis might have used the name and you not hear it?"*
> *Mr French answered, "He might."*
> *Sir Francis stated, "The admission that the name was heard of by Mr French before the first informations were taken, was a new fact."*
> *Mr French asked Hopkins, "Was it ever denied?"*
> *Hopkins refused to answer.*

Mr Bessonet stated:

> *The fact was never denied but, Mr French was so restricted on the trial, being bound to give a direct answer to a direct question that, he was not enabled to go into explanation.*

Sir Francis Hopkins stated:

> *He observed that, it would now seem that the name was mentioned to him before the informations were taken but, not actually at the time of writing them.*

Mr Bessonet:

> *Yes, but that he did not hear the name mentioned by you and besides that, Mr French conceived the question put by the court to have reference to the exact time at which the informations were taken.*

Sir Francis replied:

> *That was a most ingenious quibble and he gave the learned counsel the full tribute of his admiration for suggesting it.*

Mr Baldwin, President of the Court of Inquiry stated:

I do not take the matter in the restricted sense which Sir Francis did. If Mr French had been asked, at the trial, if he had heard the name of Brian Seery at all mentioned by Sir Francis Hopkins, before taking the first information, he would have been bound to answer the question distinctly and at once; but no such interrogatory had been put to him.

Mr Baldwin went on to say that, were he similarly circumstanced, he would have acted precisely in the same way. He thought the upshot of Mr French's answer to be this: that he did not, at any time, hear the name from Sir Francis Hopkins himself and therefore, did not put it into the information and that, even after the lodging of the information, he did not hear it from Sir Francis but from some persons in his house.

Sir Francis Hopkins:

I was not aware that such distinction would be drawn.

Mr Baldwin conceived that the expression, "at the time", included the whole conversation in the library and elsewhere. The learned president then expressed his wish that Mr Bessonet should state his view as to the distinction if any, that should be drawn as to the periods of time "before and at" the taking of the first information.

Mr Bessonet meant to contend that, prior to the signing of the informations, Mr French had heard the name of Seery mentioned freely in the library and upstairs and expressly by Mr Bookey, who said they were in search of a man of that name but, that Sir Francis Hopkins was not the man from whom he gathered either the name or the fact.

Sir Francis Hopkins said:

I hope the admission made by Mr French that he had heard the name prior to the lodging of the information, would ease the minds of that portion of the public who were of opinion that the name of Seery was not mentioned to Mr French before the information's were taken.

Mr French said:

I never concealed the fact. On the contrary, I had never accompanied the admission of it with the expression of regret that I had not been more particular on the subject although, I did everything for the best and considered that a personal identification would be preferable to any other.

Hopkins remarked:

*If that admission had been made three months ago, a great deal of
trouble would have been saved to him and to others and, a vast deal, if
not the entire of the misrepresentations and discussion in the public
journals (Liberal and otherwise) might have been avoided.*

Mr French said:

*Questions were put to me upon the trial to which I was called upon to
give an explicit answer and thus, I was denied the opportunity of
explaining matters as fully as I do at present. Subsequent to the trial, I
intimated to the government that, as my conduct might require some
explanation, I was prepared to give it.*

Mr French was then asked to state his opinions.

He replied:

*I emphatically declared that I had heard the name of Brian Seery, very
freely spoken of before the taking of the informations and that, in
answering the questions on the trial, I conceived that the questions
bearing upon that point had reference only to whether Sir Francis
Hopkins had mentioned the name to me.*

Sir Francis Hopkins expressed a wish that Mr Bookey who, Mr French said,
had cautioned him to "observe excessive caution in the framing of the
information's" should be examined.

Mr Baldwin was willing that Mr Bookey should be examined but, feared
very much that they could not command his attendance that day.

Sir Francis Hopkins said that, much as he desired to leave soon for England,
he would wait for a day or so until Mr Bookey could attend. They also had
Mr Browne to examine, upon the point as to the reason Mr French had for
omitting the name. This latter point, he considered of importance to Mr
French and valuable to the public.

Mr Baldwin said if the parties wished for any particular witnesses, whatever
could be done by the government to procure their attendance should be
done, if they only named them.

Sir Francis Hopkins desired the examination of Mr Bookey and Mr Browne
(Crown Prosecutors Clerk), and then he was satisfied.

Mr Bessonet had not the slightest wish to examine anybody. At the same
time, he did not say that it was not desirable to have confirmation of Mr
French's own statement by the gentleman named.

Wednesday, 13 May 1846 – Investigation Continued

James Washington Browne stated:

Last December, he travelled to Mullingar to assist in examining into the outrages that had been committed in that area. Mr Browne, together with Mr Seed, went to Rochfort House. They met with Sir Francis Hopkins and also saw Mr French. Before proceeding to Rochfort, Mr Browne had taken down the evidence of several witnesses in the Crown Office at Mullingar, amongst them Mr French. Browne read Mr French's statement, which asserted that Sir Francis did not state the name to him and therefore, he did not put it in the first information. He then travelled to Rochfort with Mr Seed.

At Rochfort, Mr Seed asked Sir Francis Hopkins:

To whom he first mentioned that he knew it was Seery?

Sir Francis replied:

To Dr Ferguson.

Mr Seed asked:

If you knew it was Seery who attacked you, why you did not mention his name to Mr French while giving the first information the next morning?

Sir Francis replied:

I did mention the name to Mr French.

At this stage, Mr French was not present; he arrived shortly after. In a subsequent conversation between all the parties, Mr French, to the best of Mr Browne's recollection, made a statement similar in substance to that which Browne had previously written down. Browne stated he was present at the first investigation and at the trial added:

I really believe it was an error on the part of Mr French, in having omitted Brian Seery's name while writing down the first information and, it appeared to me, the omission did not in any manner vitiate the identification of Sir Francis Hopkins.

Mr Browne added:

I do not remember to have heard it stated after Mr French entered the room, that Sir Francis had mentioned the name of Brian Seery at the time of taking the first information.

In reply to Sir Francis Hopkins, Mr Browne said:

I was under the impression that Sir Francis had mentioned the name to Mr French and that, from hurry or some other cause, he had omitted it.

In answer to Mr Bessonet, Mr Browne replied:

The impression arose from what Sir Francis had said, not what Mr French said. I thought it very natural the manner in which Sir Francis mentioned it. He spoke so positively that he had done so.

Browne continued:

I recollect Mr French telling me, he did not put down the name, Brian Seery, in the first information, for fear it might turn out not to be his Christian name and, if it was Barney or Patrick Seery, it might damage the Prosecution.

In response to Mr Bessonet, Mr Browne said:

I did not state, in the conversation at Rochfort, that Mr French had told him Sir Francis did not name Seery previous to time of making the first information.

Mr Bookey was the next witness to be called and stated:

I arrived was at Rochfort at about ten o'clock on the morning of the 19th of November. I think the first person I saw was Mr French. I had a conversation with him and communicated to him the fact that Sir Francis had been attacked. I stated to Mr French that I had received a letter from Dr Ferguson that morning, at a quarter before four, in which he mentioned that Sir Francis Hopkins suspected a man named Brian Seery for having fired at him. In consequence of that information, I sent out the police in different directions in pursuit of Brian Seery and I had Seery's house searched.

To Sir Francis Hopkins:

I was in the library at Rochfort. I heard Sir Francis detail in the presence of all assembled there, the circumstances surrounding the attack which had been made upon him. I remember Sir Francis mentioned the name of Brian Seery. Mr French was in the room at the time. I was standing at the end of a sofa on which Sir Francis was sitting. A good many gentlemen were around him. I heard Seery's name mentioned on numerous occasions. It is possible, from the position in which Mr French was placed – sitting at the end of a table about three paces from the sofa and a good many gentlemen intervening from time to time between him and Sir Francis Hopkins – that he did not hear the name Brian Seery. Under ordinary circumstances, I should say, Mr French could have heard it. Sir Francis spoke in his usual tone.

When questioned if it was probable that Mr French did not hear the name, Bookey replied:

In a conversation with Mr French the next day, Mr French told him he had not heard the name from Sir Francis Hopkins. He did from others but not from him.

Bookey went on:

The impression on my mind, before I saw Sir Francis, was that he suspected a man named Brian Seery. I do not think I told Mr French anything more than to use great caution in drawing up the informations. At the time I received the letter from Dr Ferguson, I did not think there was more than suspicion in the mind of Sir Francis against Brian Seery.
I recollect a conversation between Mr French, Mr Uniacke and Captain Vignoles. Mr French said it is a terrible business but, it is a glorious thing that Sir Francis is able to identify one of the men who attacked him and to the best of my belief he mentioned the name of Brian Seery. From the confident manner Mr French spoke, I supposed Mr French believed Seery to be the man.

In reply to Mr Baldwin:

There was nothing said by Sir Francis to lead me to think he had the least doubt about Seery; he was positive as to him. Mr French was then in the room. There were several speaking at the same time. On the 1st of December and at other times, Mr French assigned reasons for omitting the name of Brian Seery at the time of taking the first informations. Mr French always spoke as if he had not heard the name from Sir Francis but, from others.

Sir Francis Hopkins asked Mr French whether:

... when taking the informations and no name was inserted, would it not be the duty of the acting magistrate to inquire the name of the person accused?

Mr French said:

Under some circumstances, I think yes; in others, no. In the case of Sir Francis, I think I fulfilled my duty by the course I adopted. I gave the informations to Sir Francis and in doing so, he had the opportunity of reading them and making any alteration he might deem necessary. I regretted I had not asked the name as the omission had given rise to a great deal of controversy. I think it is discretionary from whom information may be taken with respect to proving the arrest of a party accused. When Sir Francis had described a tall man in the information, I believed the impression on Sir Francis's mind was that the man was Brian Seery. When I used the words glorious new – Sir Francis is able to identify, the impression on my mind was that when Sir Francis saw the man, he could identify him. I suppose the name of Brian Seery originated with Sir Francis Hopkins.

To Mr Baldwin:

I do not particularly recollect from whom I got the general description of the man as described in the information. I read the informations to the other magistrates and they agreed with me.

At this stage, the evidence closed on both sides.

Mr Baldwin, President of the investigation, commenced his summary by stating:

As no further witnesses are to be examined, we shall close the inquiry. I had the fullest instructions to make this a searching inquiry, so as to satisfy both Sir Francis Hopkins and Mr French. I have not, in any instance, trammelled the examination of witnesses by holding to restricting witnesses when the prisoner should arrive, to take a second information, stating the man to be one of the said who were referred to in the first informations.
As there was professional assistance on one side and not on the other, it was my object, as far as was consistent with my position here, to assist Sir Francis Hopkins, who was unattended by counsel. This was not required by Mr French, who was so well represented by his counsel. It will be my duty to report the evidence to his Excellency but, I think the results will be satisfactory to all parties. I am not at liberty to make known the impression on my mind now but, I may be permitted

to state, the impression on my mind at first was that the issue we had to try involved a contradiction but, that is not the case. Sir Francis stated and it is not contended here, that he had named Seery before signing the first information. When the name was omitted it, of course, formed the object of observation at the trial. Mr French says he never heard Sir Francis mention the name and this does not involve the contradiction I was, at first, prepared to think we had, at first, to meet.

The President, Mr Baldwin then closed the investigation.

~

This is very unusual to say the least. At the same time, I'm not surprised that the gentleman presiding over the investigation openly admitted to assisting Hopkins throughout the entire proceedings. While questioning Hopkins he said:

... and deponent (Hopkins) said, there is one of the men whom he would know on seeing again.

He omitted the following:

I was attacked by two unknown assailants, I could recognise one of them if I saw him again.

Furthermore, he tacitly announced the results of the investigation by saying "both sides would be satisfied with the outcome."

I failed in my endeavours to locate his Excellencies report on the issue. On studying Mr Baldwin's summary, I believe the results would have been that:

As there was no proof of contradiction, it is the decision of the Commission that:

1. Sir Francis Hopkins did mention the name of Brian Seery to Mr French before giving the first informations.
2. Due to background noise, it was impossible for Mr French to hear Seery's name being mentioned.

However, the evidence does not concur with such an outcome. In reality, the letters supporting Hopkins that were handed to the Commission contained un-sworn contradictions between the writers. The majority of the authors did not attend the Government Inquiry. The content of the letters was not checked against the evidence as sworn during the trials.

The biggest bone of contention, in my opinion, was the fact that Mr John Lyons and Mr William Reilly, while their letters were taken into consideration, were absent from the investigation. These two magistrates were in attendance while Mr French wrote down and read aloud the content of the first informations. They immediately certified the content as being correct and right. During the following weeks, after Hopkins got to Lyons, he altered the facts. He said Hopkins mentioned Seery's name while he was "having a chat" with him and, at the same time, Mr French was busy writing down the statement.

Mr Reilly wasn't called as a witness for the Prosecution because, he said he didn't hear Hopkins mention Seery's name. Mr French's defence team had no opportunity to cross-examine these people, in an attempt to discover the truth as to what transpired during the taking of the first informations. I do not accept Lyons' lame excuse concerning conversations taking place while Mr French was dealing with a very important issue. As magistrates, would they, or indeed Hopkins, tolerate such behaviour in their courts? Actually, one of Hopkins important witnesses, the Crown Prosecutor, Mr Seed stated:

If informations founded upon a private conservation, held between two gentlemen, were sworn, it would be most improper.

Dr Ferguson should also have attended the investigation. While he didn't certify the statement by way of signature, he witnessed the informations being given by Hopkins and read aloud by Mr French. No matter what the Commission decided, facts are facts and the evidence proves that Hopkins did not mention Seery's name to Mr French, before or during the time he gave his first informations.

On the first day of the Investigation, Hopkins was asked:

Whether Mr French might have heard the name?

He replied:

If busy occupied writing, I could not say what another heard.

A few minutes later, Hopkins contradicts this when he said:

It is my positive impression that Mr French heard me mention Brian Seery, previous to drawing up the first information.

However, he did not mention the fact that Mr Reilly, who was also present, did not hear Seery's name being mentioned.

The Court:

The first information states, "and deponent (Hopkins) said, there is one of the men, whom he would know on seeing again." Who was that?

Hopkins replied:

Brian Seery.

When asked:

Did you observe that statement in the information before you swore it because, that would imply that the man was not known?

Hopkins replied:

I did not remark it.

Adding,

This is all I have to state with reference to the first charge.

As Hopkins made it clear that he would answer no more questions on the first charge, I'm sure he was in contempt, as he obstructed the course of the investigation.

Hopkins also had a problem with the way Mr French answered a question during Seery's second trial. The question was:

Did Sir Francis Hopkins mention any name to you at the drawing up of the first informations?

To which Mr French replied:

No.

Mr Baldwin, President of the Court of Inquiry interrupted and stated:

I do not take the matter in the restricted sense, which Sir Francis did. If Mr French had been asked, at the trial, if he had heard the name of Brian Seery at all mentioned by Sir Francis Hopkins before taking the first information, he would have been bound to answer the question distinctly and at once but, no such interrogatory had been put to him.

He (Mr Baldwin) would say that, were he similarly circumstanced, he would have acted precisely in the same way.

Hopkins witnesses gave various reasons in their letters as to why Seery's name was omitted from the first statement, each of them saying, "that's what Mr French said."

Mr Browne admitted he heard nothing when he stated:

I was under the impression that Sir Francis had mentioned the name to Mr French and that, from hurry or some other cause, he had omitted it.

He went on to say:

The impression arose from what Sir Francis had said, not what Mr French said. I thought it very natural the manner in which Sir Francis mentioned it. He spoke so positively that he had done so.

~

Browne believed everything the "Bad Bart" had to say, simply by the way he said it. Browne, just like the rest of the prosecution witnesses, was one of Hopkins' "merry men".

~

Hopkins described the alleged attack to Dr Ferguson. Ferguson wrote everything down and handed the letter to Mr Bookey. The letter contained the following sentence:

I did not think there was more than suspicion in the mind of Sir Francis against Brian Seery.

~

Conspirators' Letters of Support

It was no coincidence that the majority of letter writers did not attend the Government investigation. Hopkins knew the contradictions enshrined in their written statements would surely be blown out of the water by the Defence. It is my belief that Hopkins put together a gang of conspirators. He wrote to anyone and everyone he thought would assist him. Most of them responded to his plea, as he endeavoured to justify his role in the execution of Brian Seery.

Two magistrates, Lyons and Reilly, were more than happy with Mr French's recording of Hopkins' evidence. However, Lyons in particular, quickly realised he was offside and, in order to play Hopkins' game, he needed to make amends by distancing himself from the truth.

In a letter to Mr French, dated 24 January 1846 (shortly after Seery's conviction), Lyons attempted to explain himself and his sworn evidence given during Brian Seery's second trial. Lyons was asked during the trial,

> *... whether all that was said by Sir Francis Hopkins was inserted in the informations?*

Lyons replied:

> *No.*

Lyons was then asked:

> *... whether the name of any person mentioned by Sir Francis Hopkins was not inserted in the informations?*

Lyons replied:

> *Yes.*

Lyons in his letter to Mr French wrote:

> *To both questions, I stated to the court that my answers required an explanation but, the court would not permit me to explain either. I therefore feel myself called on to give this explanation now, which I was heretofore prevented from giving.*

Lyons continued:

> *While I was speaking to Sir Francis Hopkins respecting the attack on him, you were sitting at a table, writing the depositions. It is probably from your being at some distance from us and occupied in writing the informations at the time, you may not have heard the conversation.*

Mr French responded:

> *I am surprised at your account of the evidence, as I was not at your examination (not being allowed into court). You state, a name was mentioned at the time the informations were being taken. Now, do you recollect my being with you at Lediston when Mr Seed arrived and, my asking you if you, at the time of the informations being taken, recollect Sir Francis Hopkins had mentioned any name and, you distinctly said, you did not. Mr Reilly told me, he did not recollect any name being mentioned by Sir Francis Hopkins at the taking of the first informations so, we were unanimous in the opinion. Dr Ferguson was the only other individual in the room, except Sir Francis and, I rather think he is of the same opinion.*

~

Four days before Seery was executed, Mr Lyons wrote to Hopkins. The content of his letter contained the following,

Neither of our county members are sufficiently men of business to meddle in it and, however willing Mr Tuite might be, his facility of speaking is not such as to enable him to make a good hand of it. Chapman might, per adventure, be asleep when he ought to be broad awake.

~

I read the above as an attempt, by Lyons, to assist Hopkins assemble a gang of conspirators consisting of men he could trust. The two named gentlemen were deemed by Lyons to be "flat tyres" and therefore, did not have the ability to play the game according to Hopkins' rules.

Obviously, the letters Hopkins mailed to potential conspirators were not handed to the Commission so, I don't know what some of them contained. However, a number of these letters, not them all, appeared in the *Westmeath Guardian* on 14 May 1846.

Mr William Reilly, the second magistrate who certified that Hopkins' evidence, as taken down by Mr French "was a true and accurate recording of what took place in Hopkins bedroom that day", also wrote a letter to Mr French. It was dated 30 January 1846. He mentioned the following:

The day Mr Seed was in Mullingar, I recall you asking me, did I hear Seery's name being mentioned by Sir Francis Hopkins. I said I did not.

Mr Reilly, in reply to a letter from Sir Frances Hopkins dated 18 February 1846, wrote the following,

I am sorry to say, I can give you but little satisfactory information on the subject you require, as I was not in Rochfort the day Mr Seed was with you. On the day after the shot was fired, I was present when Mr French took the first informations. I went to the window and was speaking to Dr Ferguson and, I did not hear the detail of the informations as you gave them. Consequently, I did not hear the name of Seery being mentioned by you. When Mr French read them out, I thought all was right. He asked me to sign and I did so.

Mr Reilly again (referring to when Mr Seed came to Mullingar):

I told him that I did I not think the omission of Seery's name would shake the jury. I also said to him that as your uncontradicted identification could not be got over and, that if your evidence was what I expected, the man must be found guilty.

~

So, now we have two magistrates – witnesses to a very important issue – stating that they were engaged with others in, if you wish, "an auld chat" during the proceedings. This, as far as Mr Lyons was concerned, was the reason Mr French did not hear Seery's name mentioned and also, Mr Reilly's excuse for not hearing the name being mentioned.

Captain Vignoles also got in on the act. He wrote to Sir Francis Hopkins on 16 February 1846. The significant sections in his letter are as follows,

Mr Uniacke has shown me your letter and requested me to put in writing, a statement of what I know, subsequent to the night of the attempt made upon your life.
I heard from Col Caulfield a few hours after the attempt having been made and, of you having named Brian Seery as the party by whom the shot was fired at you.
On the following morning, while at breakfast at Col Caulfield's with whom I was staying, Mr Uniacke came in to inform us of the occurrence, not aware of our previous intelligence.
At about eleven o'clock, Caulfield, Uniacke and I walked over to Rochfort. On entering the hall, we found Mr Bookey in it. He told us of there being a hat and coat found and, of the police being then in pursuit of Seery. From the hall, we went into the library.
Mr French was there and he said, "is not this a glorious business?"
Said I (Captain Vignoles), "Is it Sir Francis being shot at?"
French replied, "No" but, his being able to identify one of them – a man named Brian Seery – and, we have been sent out to arrest him.
Subsequently other magistrates arrived. The hat was produced, as was the coat. I brought you in to the hall to see the coat, which you had not previously seen but, which on examination, you declared knowledge of. You, afterwards, went upstairs and made your first information.

Captain Vignoles, a member of the Conspiracy Gang, contradicts some of Hopkins' evidence, as sworn during the trials, by writing the following in his letter of support:

The morning after the attack, I brought Hopkins into the hall at Rochfort House to show him the coat ...

adding,

> *... you had not previously seen the coat but, on examination, you declared knowledge of. You, afterwards, went upstairs and made your first information.*

However, while giving evidence during Seery's trial, Hopkins' swore:

> *Constable Johnston was the first who showed me the coat at five o'clock the following day.*

However, during his examination by Mr French, prior to him writing down the first and, hours later, the second informations,

> *Hopkins did not declare knowledge of either the coat or hat. He never mentioned them.*

While Dr Ferguson, another conspirator, did not confirm that "Hopkins mentioned Seery's name to Mr French," he was being economical with the truth. He should have stood up like a man and said, 'Hopkins did not mention Seery's name to Mr French.'

The famous letter, written by Ferguson at a quarter before four o'clock, Wednesday morning and handed over to the police states:

> *Hopkins suspects it was a man he ejected named Brian Seery.*

A few hours later, after Hopkins bounced Seery's name off the magistrates in the library, the suspicion morphed into a full-blown positive identification.

Also enshrined in Ferguson's letter was the following:

> *Sir Francis Hopkins told him that, during the scuffle, "the fellow's hat came off."*

However, that's not what Hopkins swore in Court. His sworn evidence during the first trial was as follows,

> *The attacker had no hat on him when I saw him.*

On 17 February (a few days after Seery's execution), Ferguson wrote to Sir Francis Hopkins and mentioned the following,

> *The odium of hanging Seery being exclusively on you and me and, perhaps equally as much on the police for **"paid swearing"** but, as it is said, "their evidence not being believed", that we are the persons who hung him."*

~

Dr Ferguson and Hopkins were coming under severe pressure from the locals. These two individuals deserved all the bullshit that was thrown at them. Hopkins, wrongly thinking that he could buy his way out of the predicament he deservedly found himself in, donated £5 to the local parochial school. He contacted the media, with the view of having word of the donation circulated throughout the county and they, in turn, published his wish on 9 July 1846. His donation didn't work, however.

It must be said that he had some neck in thinking he could make everything alright by using a young widow's money. He should have paid his debt owed to the Seery family. However, he donated absolutely nothing to the fund set up to assist the widow of the man he legally murdered. Hopkins owed Mrs Seery and her family a year's rent, as agreed with her late husband. However, the way he looked at it was, if he paid Mrs Seery the rent money due to her, that would defeat the purpose of eliminating her husband.

As a fully paid-up member of the Conspiracy Gang, Ferguson knew what he was talking about and well aware of what was going on. He knew how far Hopkins and his supporters would go to in order to murder Seery and, while all this was going on, he stood idly by. The tone of his letter is confirmation of what I already knew: this man was going through a very rough period and, I know the locals never forgave him. To this day, quite a number of Mullingar residents, old and young, still haven't come to terms with how and why the unfortunate Brian Seery was sent to an early grave.

Ferguson's letter begs the question; how many witnesses were paid to give evidence against Seery? We know the "paid witness" conspiracy gang was made up of police officers and members of Hopkins staff. Judging by some of the police evidence, especially when it came to the hat and coat, it seems these guys were in receipt of a substantial backhander to provide false evidence at the behest of the Prosecution. A number of Hopkins' employees were not behind the door either when it came to swearing a few porkies in order to assist their "master". So, who bankrolled this? Of course, it was the "Bad Bart" himself, Sir Francis Hopkins and, no doubt he used some of the money he owed the Seery family in order to murder their dad. This behaviour is akin to the Prosecution hiring a hit-man to do their dirty work. It seems to me, the Mafia was British made and assembled in Ireland with branches Empire-wide.

I spent months researching the "paid witness" section of Ferguson's letter, all to no avail. The British destroyed a lot of the paperwork concerning their illegal activities throughout the island of Ireland. However, my research did reinforce my belief that, the majority of people in authority were then and still are, rotten to the core. If you don't believe me, take a good look at the majority of our politicians and their friends, the wealthy.

Mr N. Loftus Tottenham (Hopkins' brother-in-law) in his letter to Hopkins, dated 17 February 1846, stated the following:

While at Rochfort on the 1st of December, Mr French said, in my presence, that he thought the name of Seery had been mentioned by you at the time of the taking of the first informations but, that he and the other magistrates conceived it better not to put the name in the information, lest there might be any mistake made by you as to the name, or Christian name, of the person you said you knew. Mr Lyons was also present then and gave his assent to that statement of Mr French, he (Mr Lyons) having been the other J.P. who took the informations with Mr French and, I think, Mr Lyons and he also said, they never insert the name in a first information as a general rule, and it was better not to do so.

Hopkins even lobbied the Crown and assistant Crown solicitors and they responded with an undated letter written by Mr Seed, that contained the following:

I have a perfect recollection of my stating to Mr French, in your library, that I should be sorry to undergo the cross-examination that you and he would be subjected to in the consequence of the name of Seery not having been stated in the information and that he, Mr French, did it for the best, not wishing to bind you by the mention of a name. Mr Browne, who was also present will, I have no doubt, recollect the matter also.

Believe me, dear Sir Francis,

very truly yours,

S. Seed

Mr Seed, you may recollect, was the Crown Solicitor who lobbied members of the Grand Jury prior to the commencement of Seery's second trial. In my opinion, it would be fair to say, he was a very experienced lobbyist in support of British injustice in Ireland. The wording of his letter contains a tacit threat to Mr French, warning him of the rigid cross-examination he would be subjected to during the forthcoming trial.

James Washington Browne, while he composed a letter of support for Hopkins, did give evidence during the Investigation at Dublin Castle. Browne stated:

> *I was under the impression that Hopkins mentioned Seery's name to Mr French.*

He also said:

> *I firmly believe it was a mistake on the part of Mr French, in having omitted Seery's name in the first information.*

However, Browne added:

> *I do not recollect to have heard it stated after Mr French came into the room, that Sir Francis had mentioned the name at the time of taking the first information.*

Browne also said,

> *I recollect Mr French telling me, he did not put down the name, Brian Seery, in the first information, for fear it might turn out not to be his Christian name and, if it was Barney or Patrick Seery, it might damage the Prosecution.*

This conspirator, Mr Browne, (Mr Seed's clerk), confirmed, under oath, his reason for believing Hopkins version of events was:

> *... on account of the way Hopkins spoke.*

Taking all this on board, what chance had Seery got against a gang of well-paid conspirators? We know Seery meant nothing to these people. They were even prepared, at Hopkins behest, to circle the wagons in order to plan an attack, in an attempt to destroy one of their own, Mr French.

Sub Inspector, Mr Bookey was also lobbied by Hopkins. He wrote a letter dated 16 February 1846 and stated the following:

> *I beg to state, in answer to your note, that I have a perfect recollection of going to Rochfort on the 1st of December. There were present there on that occasion, Mr French, Mr Lyons, Mr Seed, Mr Browne and myself. Mr French stated, he omitted putting Brian Seery's name in the first information, fearing there were two Brian Seerys and that, putting the name would embarrass you.*

Hopkins supporters, the letter writers, gave numerous versions as to the reason Mr French allegedly gave for omitting to enter Seery's name in the first informations. I don't think I need to repeat them but, most of these conspirators knew full well, they would not be compelled to give sworn evidence.

Hopkins lobbied all of the above and several others. When he had the audacity to contact the Crown Solicitor and the Sub Inspector, there is no doubt, in my mind, that he also lobbied Mr Baldwin Q.C., President of the Commission set up by the government to investigate the charges in relation to the conduct of Mr French.

I give credit to Mr Baldwin for backing Mr French's approach, as he answered "closed questions" while giving evidence during Seery's second trial. However, his summary at the close of the investigation goes a long way to confirm my suspicions that he discussed the case with Sir Francis Hopkins, some time prior to the commencement of the inquiry.

Mr French, while giving evidence at the Court of Inquiry stated:

> *I was the person who drew the informations. I got the general description from the groom and some others and, drew them up in the general way designedly – not wishing to pin Sir Francis to any description until a personal identification would take place.*

This came to light in May, three months after Seery's execution and, it certainly raises a red flag. This is confirmation that they, members of Hopkins staff, just like the carriage-man, Mr Pallinger, saw the assailants or, they were told by Hopkins to say they did. As Seery, from time to time, called to Rochfort House and at least three more members of staff (the groom and others) could give a description to Mr French confirming that they saw the assailants, why didn't they name Seery as one of them? This was not disclosed in evidence during the first trial and I doubt if it was mentioned during the second trial. These people knew Seery and, the Prosecution couldn't take the chance on them being aggressively cross-examined by counsel for the Defence on the issue. Judging by the performance of Mr Murphy for the Defence, I have no doubt that, if he was made aware of this, he would have cross-examined them in an aggressive manner as he fought to save Seery's life. This disclosure is one more in the litany of discrepancies, lies and withholding of evidence in order to murder an innocent man.

It was not up off the ground that Hopkins picked his ability to screw the working classes. His father was a serial offender in this area. Hopkins senior, the first baronet, was born in 1757. He was a solicitor. He settled at Athboy and was, for many years, agent to Lord Darnley. He was an active magistrate and distinguished himself, when in charge of a military unit, by dispersing a party of unfortunates, driven to desperation by outrageous laws, administered by fellows of the Hopkins stamp.

He was conferred a baronet in 1795 and he died in 1814. He was succeeded by his son, Sir Francis Hopkins Jnr, alias the "Bad Bart". When Sir Francis

Jnr died, the property reverted to his sister, Mrs Tottenham, relict of Nicholas Loftus Tottenham, Glenfarne Hall, County Leitrim. Tottenham, his brother-in-law, was a co-conspirator in the Brian Seery saga.

Rochfort House

Rochfort House (now Tudenham House). Scene of the alleged attack on Sir Francis Hopkins. Main entrance on the left.

Drive leading to what was then Rochfort House. The drive is lined with trees of every description. This, together with a number of twists and turns would make an excellent ambush site. The drive is about 300 yards long and, pitch dark at night so, why wait outside the house for Hopkins to arrive home and risk the chance of being identified by servants?

Remains of Brian Seery's Old Farmhouse

Remains of Brian Seery's farmhouse (gable end on the left, entrance on the right). The porch was added to the main building during the 1900s. In the 1840s, the property was owned by Sir Francis Hopkins, Bart. Seery was a rent-paying tenant.

Jim Bourke (Mullingar Autos) pictured outside the porch of Brian Seery's home. The farm was purchased by Jim Bourke's family during the 1950s and Jim resided on the premises as a child. Many thanks to Jim for taking me on an extensive guided tour of the farm in Rathnamuddagh, Dysart, Mullingar, Co. Westmeath

Kiernan Family Home and Stables

Front of the Kiernan family home. The extension on the left rear was added years after Brian's death.

Kiernan family house, back yard and stables. Brian Seery's uncle's premises. Brian was asleep in this house at the time of the alleged attack on Sir Francis Hopkins – eight miles from Rochfort House.

Jimmy Kiernan (one of Brian Seery's living relatives) pictured outside the stables where Brian, from time to time, assisted the Kiernan family as they tended to their horses.

Brewery Yard Homes

At the time of his arrest, Brian Seery lived in this housing development. The roofs would have been thatched at this time. I failed to discover which house the Seery family resided in. The brewery is situated opposite.

James Seery in Australia

Photos from Gippsland Gold Fields and Crooked River Mining Village, Australia.
Clockwise from top left: Gold Mine Interior; miner's hut, interior; old mining
machinery; miner's hut, exterior

Beautiful countryside, fantastic scenery. Gippsland, Victoria, Australia

Photos used courtesy of Dave Charleston, Gippsland in Pictures

Miner's hut (not exactly a five-star hotel). Gippsland, Victoria, Australia

19th century miner's hut. Crooked River, Gippsland, Australia

Photos used courtesy of Dave Charleston, Gippsland in Pictures

James Seery earned his money down in the mines

Mine entrance propped up with timber. Gippsland, Victoria, Australia. Another place of employment for James Seery.

Photos used courtesy of Dave Charleston, Gippsland in Pictures

Long tunnel extended gold mine. 19th century reports from Victoria, Australia confirm that James Seery worked on all the goldfields in Gippsland so, he must have worked here.

Mine with double entrance or, is it two separate mines? Gippsland, Victoria, Australia

Photos used courtesy of Dave Charleston, Gippsland in Pictures

Antique Mining Equipment

19th century goldmine winch. Gippland, Victoria, Australia

Miner's forge. Gippsland, Victoria, Australia

Photos used courtesy of Dave Charleston, Gippsland in Pictures

Gippsland old mining equipment

Photo used courtesy of Dave Charleston, Gippsland in Pictures

Part II

~ James Seery ~

Gippsland, Australia. 1870.

Chapter 9

James Seery's Australian Nightmare

Brian's son, James, arrived in Australia aboard the ship, *Lightening*, in 1861. He initially took up employment on a station (farm) and later worked in the mining industry. James actually worked in all the goldfields located in the Gippsland area of Australia.

On the morning of 16 September 1870, the tranquillity of the mining village of Crooked River was disturbed by the sound of timber burning and smoke engulfing the entire area. The residents quickly discovered the origin of the problem was Seery's hut. Great clouds of smoke were rising through the roof, quickly followed by long tongues of flames bellowing towards the sky. The blazing hut presented a remarkable sight however, the villagers main concern was for Seery: they didn't know his whereabouts and silently prayed that he wasn't burned to death in the inferno.

The blaze was so intense that the entire roof quickly collapsed. The neighbours were unable to enter the premises. Seery was nowhere to be seen and, at this stage, no one suspected anything sinister had taken place. A number of people entered the hut when it was safe to do so. A human skull was discovered and, the police stationed at Grant were notified.

Two days later, Constable Coleman arrived in the village to carry out an investigation. He stated that he found a human skull in the fireplace, in Seery's hut and, he later found a headless body in a shallow grave near the hut. The body was identified as that of local miner, Auguste Tepfar. All of this, together with Seery's absence, pointed the finger of suspicion in his direction. He was arrested 23 miles away, in a place close to the Twenty-Five Mile Creek.

Police Court (District Court), 6 October 1870

Seery was brought up and charged with the wilful murder of Auguste Tepfar, alias Charley Depford. The prisoner, in a clear voice, pleaded not guilty to the charge.

Peter Mentz stated:

> *I am a storeman to Mr Kreymbourg and reside at Crooked River. I know Seery and I knew the deceased. I remember the 16 September*

last. The prisoner's hut is about 30 yards below the junction of Good Luck Creek with the Crooked River. Auguste Tepfar also lived on the same side of the river. Their huts are about 300 yards apart and on the opposite side of the river to where I live. Deceased worked in Rudolph Klemptz's claim for wages and, on going to his work, had to pass Seery's hut, within a few yards. I last saw the deceased alive on the morning of the 15th. The following morning, I noticed a fire in Seery's hut and I went over to see if I could save anything. The roof had collapsed into the building. This was approximately a quarter to ten in the morning. I returned to the scene on Friday and did not enter the hut because of the heat of the fire. I could see the hut from the store. I went to the hut again on Saturday and noticed some changes. For example: saplings that were lying alongside the logs outside the hut on Friday had been removed and, apparently put on the fire; the victim had a scar on the left hand and a joint gone from one finger. I have not seen Tepfar alive since. I saw the body that was found and saw a scar on the hand similar to that on Tepfar's hand.

William Beaumont, stated:

I am a miner residing at the Crooked River and part owner of a mining claim. There was a man named Auguste Tepfar employed in the claim. On the 15 September, he was at work and left about five o'clock in the evening and went home. He was leading a horse. He would, most probably, pass Seery's hut in going home because, if he went by the lower track, there would be a dangerous cutting to pass. I was at work on the 16th but Tepfar did not come to work on that day. He was expected to come to work; I have not seen him alive since. I knew he had a joint missing off one finger and also, some scars on the hand. On Saturday, I saw the prisoner's hut on fire; it was nearly all burnt. I examined the ruins and found what appeared to be a human skull. I did not see the prisoner there. Information was given to the police and on Sunday, I accompanied them to the hut and I picked up some human teeth from the fire. The bones and teeth produced are, I believe, the same. I also saw stains of blood about the hut.
I was present when the headless body of a man was found buried in some old workings; this was about 100 yards from Seery's hut. There was a wound on the side and a jagged wound near the neck. One joint of the little finger was missing. There were also some cuts on the hand. From the marks, I could swear to the body as being that of Auguste Tepfar. The size and appearance of the body also appeared like Tepfar's. There was a shirt round the neck of the body; the one produced is the same and I have seen Seery wear one similar in appearance. I know nothing about the blanket produced; I never saw it

before. I saw a pick that was found on the bank near the body; the one produced is the same and belonged to deceased. I saw the pick with him the Sunday previous to the murder. In my opinion, the wound near the neck could have been made with a pick. I never saw deceased wear a shirt like the one produced. I know of no dispute between deceased and the prisoner. The body was quite fresh when we found it. I could not say which hand the joint of the finger was missing from. A pair of boots was found buried near the body; those produced are the same and I can swear they belonged to the victim Auguste Tepfar.

John Leavell, stated:

I am a miner and I reside at Crooked River. I remember the 15 September last. I knew the deceased, Auguste Tepfar, well and I know James Seery well. They lived on the same side of the river. I saw Seery at the junction on the 12 September last and, he was wearing a shirt very similar to that produced on the 17 September. I was at the burning hut and saw some bones of a human skull found. They were much charred, like those produced on the 18th. I saw a headless human body found about eighty yards from Seery's hut. I recognised the body as that of Auguste Tepfar from the top joint of the little finger on the right hand missing and, the thumbnail was turned in a peculiar manner and grown over the end. I also saw the headless body of a dog being taken out of a grave beside where the man's body was found. I believe it was Tepfar's dog. I last saw Tepfar alive on the 11 September. I knew of no dispute between him and the prisoner. The wound on the neck was like one that could be made by the pick produced. There were no clothes on the body.

Rudolph Klemtz stated:

I am a miner, residing at the Crooked River. I knew Tepfar; he worked for me as a miner. I last saw him alive on the 15th. He was working on that day and left about 5pm. I told him to come in early on the 16th as, I had some particular work to do. He did not come to work on the 16th. I knew Seery's hut and I was there on the 17th. The hut was then burned down. I saw a human skull found near the fireplace. I believe the bones produced are the same. I saw the headless body of a man found and, I identified it as that of Auguste Tepfar. There was a red blanket found with the body. The prisoner was living at my place for some time and he had a red and a blue blanket. The red blanket produced is like the one Seery had at that time. I last saw Seery at my claim on Wednesday, the 14 September. Tepfar had a large dog with him on Thursday when he left to go home. I have not seen it since.

Mrs Lee stated:

> *I am the wife of Henry Lee. I reside at Crooked River. I know the prisoner and I saw his hut on fire on 16 September. I did not see anyone near the hut in the morning. In the evening, between five and six o'clock, I saw a man wearing a white shirt walking in the direction of the hut. I thought it was Seery but was too far away to be certain. I did not see him leave the hut. The reason I thought it was Seery was because he was living there.*

Constable H. J. Coleman stated,

> *I am a police constable stationed at Grant. On 18 September, I proceeded to Crooked River, where a burnt-out hut was pointed out to me. I examined it and found the bones produced marked "A". When found, they formed a skull but, have since fallen to pieces. I found all the bones in the ashes of the fireplace. I saw a lot of saplings that appeared to have been placed in the position they were found in, for the purpose of kindling the fire. I saw marks of blood near the side of the hut and evidence of a struggle having taken place near an old water race, close to the hut. I also discovered a body without the head. It was identified as that of Auguste Tepfar. It was about ninety yards from Seery's hut when found. There was a clean wound in the right breast and a large jagged wound near the collarbone. I tried the depth of the wound near the collar bone with the pick produced. I found it would enter easily about one-and-a-half inches; the direction of the wound was downwards. The head was cut off, very clean, by some sharp instrument.*
> *I then went to Tepfar's hut and found the usual appearances of a digger's hut; it had no appearance of being deserted. The prisoner's hut, from Tepfar's, is about 900 yards distant. The body was wrapped in a red blanket with a shirt round the back. It was covered in about a foot of soil. It seemed to have been recently buried. I noticed a joint of the little finger on the right hand missing and, the thumbnail was discoloured and of peculiar formation. I found the pick produced on the bank; it was about three yards from the body. On the 20th, I found the body of a dog, without the head, buried near the feet of where I took out the man's body.*
> *On the 19th, Seery was brought into Grant. He was then dressed in the clothes produced. The shirts marked "K" and "L" are the ones he had on at that time. On the shirt marked "K", I saw marks of what appeared to be blood; the shirt had been taken off him by force.*
> *The prisoner said, "What do you want my shirts for?"*

I pointed out to him the blood marks on the shirt. I told him he was charged with the murder of Auguste Tepfar. The prisoner replied, "Who is to prove it?"

In response to the bench:

The body was found south of the prisoner's hut and, the struggle appears to have taken place between the hut and the place where the body was found.

William Lloyd stated:

I am a mounted constable and stationed at Grant. On the 18 September, I was despatched to look for Seery, or Tepfar. I came across Seery between Fraser's Restaurant and the Twenty-Five Mile Creek; the distance from Seery's hut to the place where I saw him is about 23 miles. I first saw him on the top of the spur. I had been in to the Twenty-Five Mile Creek and was coming up again; he (Seery) was going down. When he saw me, he started to walk quickly in my direction. He put down his swag and took a long-handled shovel that he had been carrying in both hands and, ran quickly towards me, in a ferocious manner. I had not spoken to him. When I was about twelve-paces from Seery, I called on him to surrender. I was in uniform at the time.
The prisoner said, "I'll teach you to come before me. I will split your bloody skull."
He then rushed at me, dealing blows right and left with the shovel. I had my revolver and fired at one side of him to try and intimidate him. He still continued to strike at me in a ferocious manner. I then dropped my revolver, dodged a severe blow he made at me and rushed at him. We closed and rolled on the ground together, the prisoner making a desperate attempt to get at my throat. I then got assistance and had him secured.
Seery said, "What are you talking to me for?"
I told him, "On suspicion of the murder of Charley Tepfar."
He said, "What suspicion can you have of me?"
He then told me, he would have taken me off my pins quick only for my dammed dodging. While at Fraser's, he said he did not care for my dammed pistol for, if I had put half a dozen holes into him, he would have murdered me if he could. Neither the prisoner nor myself lost any blood in the struggle. The shirts marked "K" and "L" are those Seery wore when arrested and afterwards, taken off him in the gaol.

Inspector Sadler, who conducted the case for the Prosecution, said this was the case for the Crown. The prisoner declined to ask any questions and was cautioned by the bench in the usual manner. When asked if he had any statement to make or, any evidence to call for his defence, merely said, "I deny the charge and have no evidence to call."

The prisoner was then committed to take his trial at the next Circuit Court, to be held at Sale.

Chapter 10

James Seery – Sale Circuit Court

James Seery, a thirty-three-year-old Irishman, was charged with the murder of Auguste Tepfar on 16 September 1870. Tepfar was described as "an honest, quiet inoffensive man" of German descent. At the time of his death, he was employed by Rudolph Klemtz at Good Luck Creek. He failed to turn up for work that morning however, nobody passed remarks on his absence until a hut, inhabited by Seery, was discovered in flames. Seery's hut was examined the following morning and, among the smouldering embers, a skull was found. At this stage nobody knew of Seery's whereabouts.

Constable Coleman, a police officer stationed at Grant was sent for, on arrival at Crooked River he immediately began to search the surrounding area. Coleman stated that he discovered the headless corpse of the victim in a shallow grave, covered with some freshly turned earth. The body had a deep stab wound on the left-hand side. He believed it was inflicted by a large knife and this in itself, according to the authorities, was sufficient to cause death. The police believe that Seery, in order to avoid detection, stripped the victim naked and burned his head and clothes. The scene of the crime was located in and around Seery's hut. Adding to the fact that he was missing, the police suspected him straight away.

Constable Lloyd followed Seery's tracks up to the Twenty-Five Mile Creek and arrested him near the house of Mr Fraser. While detained at the Grant lock-up, Seery violently resisted, his shirt being taken away, which Lloyd said was covered with blood. Several little parcels of gold and money were found on his person and, according to the police, belonged to the victim.

Seery pleaded not guilty on the charge of the murder of Auguste Tepfar at Grant, Crooked River. He was represented by Mr Patten.

Rudolph Klemtz, who resides at Crooked River, stated that Tepfar had been employed by him up to the 15 September. On that day, he left the claim at about 5pm. He was due to return early to work the next morning. Klemtz was at Seery's hut on the 19th and saw that it was burned down. He found a human skull near the fireplace and believed the bones produced to be the same. He immediately identified the headless body that was found as Auguste Tepfar's. A red blanket found with the body was similar to the one which Seery, the defendant, had in his possession when living with witness. Seery was last seen at witness's claim on Wednesday, 14 September. Since the discovery of Tepfar's body, the witness stated that he had never again seen Tepfar's large dog.

Mr Kreymbourg stated that he knew both the prisoner and the deceased and, he recalled the 16 September last. James Seery's hut was about 30 yards below the junction of Good Luck Creek with the Crooked River. Auguste Tepfar lived on the same side of the river to where the witness lived. The deceased worked on Klemtz's claim for wages and, on going to his work, had to pass Seery's hut within a few yards. The last time he saw the deceased alive was on the morning of Thursday the 15th.

On the morning of Friday, the 16th, he saw a fire in Seery's hut and went over to see if he could save anything. The roof of the hut was burnt and had fallen in. This was about a quarter to ten in the morning. He did not go again to the hut on Friday and did not go into the hut because the fire was too hot.

On Saturday, he returned to the hut and saw some difference: some saplings that were lying alongside the logs outside the hut on Friday, had been removed and, apparently put on the fire. The deceased had a scar on the left hand and a joint missing from one finger. He had not seen Tepfar alive since. He saw the body that was found and saw a scar on the hand similar to that on Tepfar's hand.

Two miners, respectively named as Beaumont and Leavell, stated that on the afternoon of 16 September, they went to Seery's hut. It was on fire and nearly burnt to the ground. They searched the hut and found what seemed to be a human skull. Seery was not there. The police were contacted and Beaumont visited the hut again, in their company and he picked up some teeth near the fire. Marks of blood were seen about the hut.

The headless body of a man was found buried in some old workings, about 100 yards from Seery's hut. There was a wound in the side and a jagged wound near the neck. From the marks on the deceased body the witness knew it was Tepfar and the shirt found with the deceased was like one that Seery used to wear. Beaumont said he was certain that the deceased had never worn a shirt of similar appearance. A pair of boots (produced) was found buried near the body on the bank and not far from the body, a pick belonging to the dead man was also found. Leavell identified the body from the fact that the top joint of the little finger on the right hand was gone. The body of a dog, known to be Tepfar's, was found near the deceased's body.

Constable Coleman stated:

> *On Sunday, 18 September, I proceeded to Crooked River where a*
> *burnt hut was pointed out to me. I examined the hut and found a*

number of bones produced, marked "A." When found, they formed a skull but have since fallen to pieces. I found all the bones in the ashes of the fireplace. I saw a lot of saplings that appeared to have been placed in the position they were found for the purpose of kindling the fire. I saw marks of blood near the side of the hut; there was evidence of a struggle having taken place near an old water race close to the hut. I also discovered a headless body. It was identified by the locals as that of Aguste Tepfar. It was found in a shallow grave about 90 yards from Seery's hut.

Coleman added:

There was a clean wound in the right breast and a large jagged wound near the collarbone. I measured the depth of the wound near the collarbone with the pick produced and discovered it would enter easily, for about one-and-a-half inches. The direction of the wound was downwards. The head was cut off very clean by some sharp instrument. I then went to the victim's hut and found the usual appearance of a diggers hut. It had no appearance of being deserted. The prisoner's hut is about four hundred yards from Tepfar's. The body was wrapped in a red blanket with a shirt placed around the back. The body was buried in about a foot of soil. It seemed to have been only recently been buried. I noticed a joint of the little finger on the right hand being missing and, the thumbnail was discoloured and of peculiar formation. I found the pick produced on the bank about three yards from the body.

Coleman continued:

On Tuesday the 20th, I discovered the headless body of a dog. It was buried near to the feet of where I took out the body of the man. On Monday the 19th, Seery was brought into Grant. He was then dressed in the clothes produced. The shirts marked "K" and "L" are the ones he had on at the time. On the shirt marked "K", I saw marks of what appeared to be blood. The shirts had to be taken off him by force.
Seery said, "What do you want my shirts for?"
I pointed out to him the blood marks on the shirt. I told him he was charged with the murder of Auguste Tepfar.
Seery replied, "Who is to prove it?"
The body was found south of the prisoner's hut. The struggle appears to have taken place between the hut and the place where the body was found.

William Lloyd deposed:

*I am a mounted constable stationed at Grant. On Sunday, 18
September, I was sent to look for Seery and Tepfar. I came across
Seery between Fraser's restaurant and the Twenty-Five Mile Creek.
The distance from Seery's hut to the place where I saw him is about 23
miles. He was then on top of the spur. I had been into the Twenty-Five
Mile Creek and was coming up again and, the prisoner was going
down. As soon as he saw me, he started to run quickly in my direction.
He dropped his swag and took a long-handled shovel he was carrying
in both hands. He ran quickly towards me in a ferocious manner. At
this stage I had not then spoken to him. When I was within about
twelve paces, I called on him to surrender. I was in uniform.
Seery said, "I'll teach you to come before me; I will split your bloody
skull."
He then rushed at me, dealing blows left and right with the shovel. I
had my revolver and discharged a shot at one side of him, in an
attempt to intimidate him. He still continued to strike at me in a
ferocious manner. I suddenly dropped my revolver on the ground,
dodged a blow he made at me and rushed him. We closed and rolled
on the ground together, Seery, making a desperate attempt to get at my
throat. I got assistance and had him secured.
Seery then said, "Why are you asking me?"
I replied, "On suspicion of the murder of Charley Tepfar."
He said, "What suspicions? I know nothing about any murder,"
adding, "I would have taken you off your pins quick only for your
dammed dodging."*

Lloyd continued:

*While at Fraser's, Seery said he did not care for my dammed pistol for,
if I had shot him a half a dozen times, he would have murdered me if
he could. Neither Seery nor myself lost any blood in the struggle. The
shirts marked "K" and "L" are the ones Seery wore when arrested
and afterwards taken off him in the Gaol.*

William Johnson, Government Analytical Chemist, said that as far as he
was able to judge, the blood spots on the shirt were human. However, he
would not swear to it adding that, there is a strong resemblance between the
blood of a dog and that of a man.

Dr Forbes proved that some of the bones produced were human but, he was
not able to identify the teeth as such.

The Prosecutor stated the case for the Crown was now closed.

Chapter 11

James Seery's Defence

Mr Patten, for the Defence, addressed the jury. He informed them that he could not help feeling a weight of responsibility in being called upon to defend the prisoner at the bar. He added, it was to be regretted that Seery was deprived of the aid of a skilled counsellor to plead his case and, he would only express the hope that the unfortunate defendant would not be punished as a result of any oversight or want of ability on the part of his advocate.

He next attempted to bring the jury onside when he said:

> *... the problems, as I see them, were somewhat lessened on this occasion because, I noticed on the jury, mainly gentlemen who had frequently sat in that box, in the court, before men of intelligence and experience and, who were therefore less likely to be led astray by anything they might have heard or, read out of doors. It would be their duty to confine themselves strictly to the evidence – the evidence they have heard during the trial – and, to come to a conclusion on that evidence and on that alone, putting aside entirely anything they might have heard or read or, any impression that may have crossed their minds before they entered upon their present solemn and responsible duty.*

Mr Patten went on:

> *James Seery was charged with the wilful murder of Auguste Tepfar and, the evidence that had been produced by the Crown in support of that charge was completely of a circumstantial nature. However, before the jury could convict his client, they must be perfectly clear in their own minds: first of all, that Auguste Tepfar was really dead; secondly that he was murdered and thirdly, that he was murdered and could have been murdered by no other person than the prisoner, James Seery.*

He added that "there was no satisfactory evidence before the court that Tepfar was not actually still living" and, in his humble judgement, the case for the Crown was weak on that point.

> *The Prosecution failed to establish the cause of the death of the body found and, whether it was that of Tepfar or not. The Crooked River was a wild and unsettled country; the wandering habits of the miner were well known. It is common knowledge, from the very nature of their occupation, that they were almost entirely their own masters, with full liberty to come and go, when and where they pleased. It was very easy for a man to be suddenly missed from such a neighbourhood, without anybody knowing his whereabouts.*

Patten added:

> *So far as the evidence went to show the contrary, Auguste Tepfar might, at that moment, be alive and well and, walking about, following his occupation in some far-off locality and, maybe residing in another part of the colony.*

This brought him to the second point, suppose the jury did not take the view of the defence case, that he had just put and were satisfied that Tepfar was really dead, where was the proof that he was murdered? The case for the Crown, he said,

> *... was very weak at this point. A headless corpse had been found and certain wounds on the trunk were sworn to. It seems strange that the Crown did not see to it that, a competent medical man was dispatched to the spot to carry out an examination, with a view of establishing if there was a connection between Tepfar, the head which was found in a half-consumed hut and, the body which was found in another place some 100 yards off.*

There was, he repeated:

> *... no evidence of mortal wounds or, whether those wounds had been inflicted before or after death and, might not decapitation have been performed after death? Might not the unfortunate man, whoever he was, have died in the bush and might not some person, who perhaps had a spite against him, have mutilated and decapitated the body?*

As to the identity of James Seery as the murderer of Auguste Tepfar,

> *... the Prosecution depended solely upon the evidence and this, of course, they must do in arriving at a verdict.*

There was a total absence of motive and, he would ask their careful attention to this point as, in all such cases, "it was of the highest importance."

In his opening speech, the learned Crown Prosecutor had certainly suggested, as a motive for the crime, that Seery had invaded a claim held by Tepfar and, wanted to keep possession of it but, that idea had been entirely upset by the evidence of the first witness called for the Crown. There was no evidence of high words or anything of the nature of a quarrel between them or, even a dispute. Tepfar was not supposed to have been wealthy and, in the absence of any direct evidence that he was, they might well conclude that he was not, for diggers, generally speaking, were most improvident and, only in a few instances, were they known to put anything aside for a rainy day.

> *If you, members of the jury, decide that the man was murdered, why was he murdered and, why should suspicion be necessarily attached to Seery and no other person? These were points to which the jury would have to give their most earnest attention and, at the same time, remember that the life of the prisoner was, to a certain extent, in their hands and, he had no fear but, they would do so.*

He pleaded with them to remember that the case for the Crown was very unsatisfactory and inconclusive in the first two issues he had put before them. On the first, as to the identity of the body as that of Tepfar, the evidence was extremely weak and incomplete. On the second, the cause of his death, he repeated again, that the learned Crown Prosecutor had not brought forward any evidence that was absolutely reliable that the man was murdered at all.

Now, unless the jury were perfectly clear in their own minds that these two points were established beyond the possibility of a doubt, they were absolutely powerless to convict James Seery. If there was even a shadow of a doubt in their minds, however small, they were bound to give the prisoner the benefit of it. He had only now to leave the case to the jury, feeling that he had defended the prisoner to the best of his ability. He had every confidence that the jury members would keep in mind the solemn responsibility resting upon them and, come to a verdict on the evidence now before them and, upon that evidence alone.

His Honour, the Chief Justice, in summing up remarked:

> *The jury had been told by the counsel for the Defence and, in his opinion, very properly, that they must be satisfied as to the identity of the body of Auguste Tepfar and that he was murdered, for those two points were clearly included in the indictment against the prisoner.*

He then carefully reviewed the evidence at some length, separating and distinguishing the minor and comparatively unimportant links from the more direct and prominent items tending to identify the prisoner as the murderer. He remarked, to the jury, that the evidence presented three questions for their consideration.

> *First, was the body found that of Auguste Tepfar? Second, was he murdered? And third, who murdered him?*

The evidence for the Crown might perhaps have been more complete as to identity, particularly as to the medical testimony but then, witnesses who knew Tepfar swore to peculiar marks about his hands and body. His clothing and tools were identified by witnesses, whose testimony seemed clear enough and this part of the evidence was not challenged by the Defence.

The second point, being the manner of his death. If he had not been murdered, why should the body have been found with such frightful wounds? Wounds that, in all probability, from their position and extent, would inevitably cause death. Then again, why was the head taken off and burnt? The fire described in Seery's hut was certainly no ordinary fire used for domestic purposes. The stonework forming the inner lining of the slabs was so heated that it ignited the timber outside. Surely, evidence such as that made it clear that the victim was murdered by somebody. What could have been the object in removing and consuming the head? It was to destroy identity. Why seek to prevent identity except, to hide evidence of murder?

Much stress had been laid upon the fact that there was an absence of evidence on the part of the Crown, as to the motive for the commission of the crime charged against the prisoner. That certainly was so but, the jury were not to assume that because no motive was apparent, therefore, no murder had taken place. And if they were satisfied that the whole chain of strong circumstantial evidence against the prisoner, proving the case for the Crown, link by link, as had been submitted to them, the question of motive was unimportant. They were to give great consideration to all the surrounding circumstances, from the discovery of the prisoner's hut in flames and the finding of the body, down to the time of his arrest and encounter with the police.

The judge continued:

> *Well, gentlemen! After a thorough consideration of the points against the prisoner and of those in his favour too, what do you make out of these circumstances? Are they consistent with his evidence? You are not required to speculate on extreme improbabilities but simply, as reasonable rational men, to weigh the evidence now before you and, upon that evidence, to find a verdict of guilty or not guilty.*

When the judge completed his unfavourable summary, insofar as the defendant was concerned, the jury retired and after an absence of about forty-five minutes, returned to the court with a guilty verdict.

In reply to the usual question of the Associate (member of the judge's personal staff) as to why sentence of death should not be passed upon him, the prisoner, who appeared shocked, was silent. The judge then proceeded to pass sentence. He said:

James Seery, you have been convicted of the wilful murder of Auguste Tepfar, on evidence which must satisfy every person who heard the trial, that the jury could come to no other conclusion.

What the motives were, that induced you to take the life of the unfortunate man, are known to yourself. There may have been some secret grudge or other cause that the trial has not brought to the surface.

It is, at times, usual on these occasions for the judge to address some remarks to the prisoner on the awful nature of the crime of which he has been convicted. However, I refrain from doing so and for this reason, that the carrying out of the sentence of the law, which it becomes my duty to pass upon you, does not rest with me but, with the Executive Council. I can find nothing in my notes which call for special comment now but, they will be forwarded at once to the Executive Council and, there is no doubt they will receive the most careful attention.

Nothing now remains for me to do but, to pass upon you the last dread sentence of the law, which is that you, James Seery, be taken hence to the place from which you came, thence to the place of execution where, on a day to be hereafter appointed by his Excellency the Governor, you be hanged by the neck until your body is dead and may the Lord God have mercy upon your soul.

Chapter 12

The Evidence

The mining village of Crooked River was a settlement where everybody knew everybody and, as such, they knew each other's business. The huts were in sight of each other: Mrs Lee could see Seery's hut from her home; Mr Kreymbourg could see Seery's hut from his place of employment. It would be very difficult to do anything, let alone slaughter a man and his large dog, without some of the neighbours noticing.

The evidence leads me to believe the murder didn't take place in or near Seery's hut or indeed, in any other part of the Crooked River village. However, the victims – the man and his dog – were beheaded in the vicinity of Seery's hut. Think about it, how could a lone attacker kill a man while his pet, a large dog, looked on? Or, how could the same man, on his own, kill a large dog, in his master's presence, without making a sound? How could all this be done in silence? The neighbours would certainly hear the dog launch an attack on the assailant. A dog, by his nature, will fight to the death to protect its master. However, there was no evidence whatsoever on Seery's body or clothes to suggest that he was attacked by a dog.

The word motive was mentioned a few times during the trial but, no one looked for a reason as to why the dog was killed. It's very simple to figure this out. The dog was killed because he launched a vicious attack in defence of his master – there was no danger of him going to the nearest police station to grass them (the killers) up. A lone man could have shot the dog however, if he used a gun, the gunshot would have wakened the entire village. Was the man or dog killed first? No matter which: a lone assailant, while doing so, had a massive problem while attacking his first victim. The dog was not the only problem the killers encountered: Auguste Tepfar, according to the prosecution witnesses, was armed with a pick.

Tepfar and his dog, without a shadow of a doubt, were killed a number of miles from the village and killed by at least two attackers. The killers knew full well that Seery had left the village to travel to Twenty-Five Mile Creek. Seery, who worked on every goldfield in the area, would know most of the miners in these fields. He could have met with the assassins on his way to Twenty-Five Mile Creek and, as he knew them, there is a possibility that he informed them of his intentions. As these people continued their journey, they came across Tepfar, his dog and horse. Shortly before the Tepfar murder, the police released, to the press, the following statement:

> *There are two or three dangerous, demented persons at large in the area.*

These gentlemen were at large in the area at the time Tepfar was killed and yet, they weren't even considered as persons of interest. Who were they? Who, or what, were they on the run from? Why were they labelled by the police as "dangerous and demented persons"? These gentlemen obviously earned that title – they certainly weren't engaged in missionary work.

The court was told by the judge and the Crown Prosecution that the police couldn't come up with a motive for the murder of Auguste Tepfar. The judge went on to say:

> *... the jury were not to assume that, because no motive was apparent, therefore no murder had taken place.*

What did he mean by that? A body was found with fatal injuries: of course, the jury knew a murder had taken place. The issue of a motive or lack of one couldn't change that. What this man was really saying to the jury was, 'it doesn't matter whether or not Seery had a motive and it's not up to the police to look for one'.

However, the horse I believe, was one of the reasons for the attack and murder of Auguste Tepfar. A horse was a valuable commodity at that time, either to sell on or keep for their own use.

A second motive was the victim himself. What was his real name? We know he used an alias. Was his name Auguste Tepfar or Charley Depford? Why would he deem it necessary to use an alias? Was he on the run from the law and if so, what type of crime was he suspected of committing? Did he escape from custody? Using an alias, at that time, was very common among desperate men. However, I suspect none of these. What I believe is, Tepfar knew his killers before he ever arrived at Crooked River. He double-crossed them someway or other. He probably informed the police about their activities or simply stole their gold or cash or, maybe killed a friend. Whatever he was guilty of was serious enough for him to hightail it as far away as possible from these men, change his name and look for employment elsewhere.

Seery was brought up at the Police Court (District Court) and charged with the wilful murder of Auguste Tepfar, alias Charley Depford. While giving evidence at this court concerning the arrest of Seery, Constable William Lloyd stated that Seery asked him:

What are you asking me for?

To which, Lloyd replied:

On suspicion of the murder of Charley Tepfar.

(While he didn't mention the surname "Depford", he certainly used half of the alias.)

He repeated this at the Sale Circuit Court. This proves that the police knew Auguste Tepfar was an alias and they knew full well why he used it. It also leads me to believe that the victim was a police informer, who had been given a new identity by the authorities and moved to a new location.

Without a doubt, the killers knew of Seery's absence and also, where he lived. They decided to take advantage of the situation and use Seery's hut to throw the blame in his direction. They worked in the dark of night as they set fire to Seery's hut, in order to destroy the victim's skull and some of his clothes. (The head could have been burned in the stove and no one would be the wiser but, if Seery set fire to his hut, he would know full well that this would draw attention before the head was destroyed, thereby risking the chance of a murder charge and execution).

The killers left behind incriminating evidence designed to prove an innocent man guilty of their crime while, at the same time, a number of people in the village, together with the police went straight to where the body was buried. Was this by accident or design?

The police stated that Seery removed the victim's head and clothes in an attempt to destroy the identity of the victim. I don't subscribe to this for a number of reasons. First of all, a man with a deformed hand goes missing and at the same time a headless body with a similarly deformed hand turns up in the village – you don't need to be a Sherlock Holmes to figure out the identity of the victim. Secondly, if, as the police stated, Seery wanted to destroy the identity of the body by burning the victim's head and clothes, if so, why didn't he remove and burn the hands and why would he bury his own clothes and blanket with the victim? This, of course would certainly place him on top of the suspect list, even if the body couldn't be identified.

During his summary, the judge deliberately informed the jury that he believed every word Constable Lloyd said about the arrest. Lloyd actually said there was at least one witness to the arrest but, where was this witness? The facts don't support Lloyd's story. The judge said that the jury were,

> *... to give great consideration to all the surrounding circumstances: from the discovery of Seery's hut in flames to the finding of the body, to the time of his apprehension and encounter with the police.*

He contradicted the police when he said:

Tepfar's clothing and tools were identified by witnesses.

While, at the same time, the police said:

In order to avoid detection, Seery stripped the victim naked and burned his head and clothes.

Giving evidence at the Police Court, Peter Mentz stated that, between a quarter to ten on Friday morning and Saturday morning, somebody removed saplings from beside some logs and placed them on the fire. Unbelievably, giving evidence at the Circuit Court, Constable Coleman said he saw the saplings on the Sunday and, he believed they were put there for the purpose of kindling the fire. This begs the question, how were the saplings still on the fire on Sunday? As for the fact they were placed on the fire, who put them there? Seery wasn't in the village so, who had an interest in kindling the fire.

Mentz also stated that the victim's hut was about 300 yards from Seery's. Constable Coleman stated (at the Police Court) the distance to be 900 yards. While giving evidence at the Circuit Court, this policeman changed his estimation to 400 yards. Why was there such a discrepancy in this man's evidence?

Three people claimed to have found the human skull in Seery's fireplace. William Beaumont stated, at the Police Court, that he found the skull when he entered Seery's hut on Saturday, 17 September. While giving evidence at the Circuit Court, he claimed he found the skull on Friday, 16 September. This man's evidence about the day he entered Seery's hut and found the skull is contradictory.

Rudolph Klemtz, while giving evidence at the Police Court, stated that he saw the skull found on 17 September. At the Circuit Court he stated:

I was at Seery's hut on the 19 and saw that it was burned down. I found a human skull near the fireplace.

This is another contradiction.

Constable Coleman stated:

On 18 September, I proceeded to the Crooked River, where a burnt hut was pointed out to me. I examined it and found the bones produced marked "A". When found, they formed a skull but have since fallen to pieces.

So, who found the skull and when was it found?

Constable Lloyd, who introduced himself as a Mounted Constable, gave an unbelievable account of what transpired while he was arresting Seery. He led the courts to believe that he was some sort of superhuman being; unfortunately, he got away with it. He said he confronted Seery, a man whom he believed had, on his own, butchered the victim and his large dog. He alleged that Seery commenced running/rushing at him while ferociously swinging a shovel.

He added,

> *I had my revolver and fired at one side of him to intimidate him. He still continued to strike at me in a ferocious manner. I dropped my revolver, dodged a blow he made at me and rushed him. We closed and rolled on the ground together.*

Lloyds account just doesn't make sense. We have, according to the authorities, a maniac running at an armed police officer. The officer fires his gun and deliberately misses. He next drops his gun and takes on this lunatic who was still ferociously swinging a shovel and, unbelievably, the lunatic failed to land a single blow. Finally, he adds, that neither he nor the killer lost blood during the encounter. Why would he say that? Was he worried that his unbelievable story would be questioned and attempted to clarify the situation first? Or, was he informing the court that the spots of blood were on Seery's shirt prior the alleged struggle?

I believe Lloyd perjured himself when he gave evidence about the bloodstains. He said Seery's shirt was covered with blood. Constable Coleman swore that there were stains on Seery's shirt that appeared to be blood so, Coleman wasn't sure. William Johnson, Government Analytical Chemist, swore that:

> *... as far as I was able to judge, the blood spots on the shirt were human but, I would not swear to it.*

Lloyd stated that he got assistance as he struggled with Seery. In other words, he had at least one witness to swear that the incident had taken place. Who was this person who assisted him as he arrested Seery? Where is this person's statement and, why did this witness not appear in court? If what Lloyd said were true, this person would have a lot more constructive evidence concerning the case than Mrs Lee for example, Mrs Lee's contribution was simply,

> *... on the evening of the 16th, I saw a man with a white shirt going towards Seery's hut. I thought it was Seery because he lived there but, he was too far off to be certain.*

Any right-thinking person would come to the conclusion that no such struggle had taken place during the arrest. Incidentally, Lloyd introduced himself as a "Mounted Constable" and as such, there is no way he walked 23 miles through the wilderness and back as he searched for Seery. However, he failed to mention the fact that he was on horseback when they met. An armed, mounted policeman has a massive advantage over an unarmed fugitive on foot. This enforces my belief that no struggle took place between Lloyd and Seery.

Another thing that bothers me is the fact that the victim's horse was missing, no doubt if Seery had committed the crime, he would have ridden off into the sunset. He wouldn't be found 23 miles away (riding the horse would probably add another forty or fifty miles to that); he would never be found. Unbelievably, Lloyd was awarded the sum of £5, paid out of the Police Reward Fund for his services while arresting James Seery. This was normal procedure and it encouraged police officers to compose a heroic tale of some sort in order to qualify for the award and, unbelievably, they were not required to produce witnesses.

The prosecution expert witness said there were spots of blood on Seery's clothes. This doesn't tie in with the facts. The police alleged Seery killed and beheaded a man and a large dog. They also allege he was involved in a ferocious struggle with a police constable. It's only reasonable to conclude that, if on his own, Seery was involved in a bloody battle to overcome man and dog and, to come out of it without a scratch or bruise on his body and, only "spots of blood" on his clothes, is stretching the truth a bit too far. The expert also stated, "I couldn't swear that the blood spots were of human origin.

The Prosecution failed to establish Seery's motive for killing Tepfar. He didn't end up with the victim's horse and not one of the neighbours knew of any dispute or animosity between Seery and Tepfar. Seery hadn't a gun, nor had he access to a crossbow. He was not in possession of the "sharp implement" the police stated was used to behead Tepfar. In reality, Seery never carried a weapon nor was he armed when arrested. He was just a miner trying to earn his fortune.

The jagged wound found near the victim's neck was, according to police, caused by the pick. In all honesty, how can that be said after Constable Coleman admitted he stuck the pick into the wound and, in doing so, contaminated evidence.

Mr Patten, in addressing the jury for the Defence, said he regretted that he hadn't the necessary skills to assist Seery plead his case and, he would only express the hope that the unfortunate man would not suffer through any oversight or want of ability on his part. Seery's life was at stake. It's unbelievable that the authorities saw fit to appoint an inexperienced or unqualified lawyer to defend him.

After reading Mr Patten's address to the jury, I concurred with him when he stated that he hadn't the experience to properly defend Seery. While he touched on the fact that the crime may not have been committed anywhere near Seery's hut or indeed, the Crooked River village, he failed to dig deeper into this assumption.

Crooked River is situated in the wilds, miles from civilisation and surrounded by wilderness. This begs the question, why would Seery kill on his own doorstep and burn his own hut, together with the victim's head and clothes?

Another question that should have been asked was, why would he bury the torso wrapped in his own shirt and blanket? If he attacked Tepfar and his large dog outside his own hut, the barking of the dog would awaken the dead and Tepfar, who was carrying a pick, wouldn't be quiet either. Tepfar was definitely murdered in the bush, miles away from Seery's hut and, you don't have to be a Sherlock Holmes to figure out, it was not a one-man job.

There were numerous anomalies in the prosecution case that the Defence should have probed in a constructive manner however, through lack of experience, Mr Patten failed to do so. Under the circumstances, I think it's fair to say, Mr Patten did his best to save Seery's life. Incidentally, Seery had no legal representation whatsoever when he appeared at the Police Court.

The judge, while addressing the court, said:

> *Witnesses who knew Tepfar, swore to peculiar marks about his hands and body. His clothing and tools were identified by witnesses whose testimony seemed clear enough and this part of the evidence was not challenged.*

On the one hand, the Prosecution stated that Seery burned Tepfar's clothes in an attempt to avoid detection and at the same time, the judge stated,

> *Tepfar's clothing and tools were identified by witnesses.*

In the real world, the first thing a killer would do, time permitting, is remove all traces of self-incriminating evidence from the murder scene, not bury his property with the victim. The vast majority of killers don't purposely leave evidence akin to a calling card however, some serial killers leave a little evidence to annoy the police.

The judge went out of his way to instil in the minds of the jury members his opinion, which, of course, was that Seery was guilty. He asked why was the victim's head taken off and burnt? He spoke about the heat intensity of the fire in Seery's hut and said it was certainly no ordinary fire used for domestic purposes. Next, he said the stonework forming the inner lining of the slabs was so heated that it ignited the timber outside. What had all that got to do with proving that Seery was the killer. Certainly, it would make him a person of interest but, that's a million miles from proving guilt.

If his summary were balanced and fair it would certainly go a long was to warrant a not guilty verdict. This man let the jury know, in his opinion "Seery was guilty", simply by failing to mention discrepancies in the Crown's case that would favour a dismissal of all charges. He finished off with the following,

> *Well, gentlemen, after a thorough consideration of the points against the prisoner and of those in his favour too, what do you make out of these circumstances? Are they consistent with his evidence? The judge failed to mention any points in favour of Seery.*

Just to recap on the conclusions I have reached as I studied this unfortunate episode, where a second member of the Seery family met an early death at the hands of the British:

The Defence should have picked up on the following:

(A) The horse as the motive. This animal was never again seen in the village after Aguste Tepfar was killed.

(B) Tepfar saw the need to use an alias. Alarm bells should have rung out here. It's a known fact that, when a man hides his identity, he has enemies, be it the police or former colleagues etc. (Were these the dangerous, demented men who, according to the police, were on the run at the time of Tepfar's murder.

(C) Why did the defence team overlook the fact that the police ignored their own press release? They informed the public that there were two or three dangerous, demented persons at large in the area?

(D) The Prosecution suggested that the parcels of gold found in Seery's possession were Tepfar's property and, Seery may have killed him in order to rob his gold and take over his claim. However, Tepfar (or Depford) was employed by Rudolph Klemtz. As a digger, he worked for wages; he wasn't a prospector and had no claim. Tepfar would not be carrying around gold unless he stole it and if so, he would have kept this quiet.

(E) Killing Tepfar in the presence of his large dog would cause such a racket that, it would have been heard at least a mile away.

(F) Killing the dog first would also create a lot of roaring and barking – enough to waken the dead. If the dog was attacked first, a lone killer would have been battered by Tepfar, who was armed with a pick. The dog was certainly killed because, he viciously attacked the assailants.

(G) Tepfar and his dog were attacked miles from the village and, more than one man was involved. Mr Patten touched on this but, he should have dug deeper.

(H) Patten should have corrected the judge and the Prosecution when they informed the court that, "Seery destroyed the victim's head and property (clothes) so as to make it difficult to identify."

The judge contradicted this in his summary when he said, "witnesses identified the victim's body and property, adding, they also identified Seery's clothes, that were buried with the body."

Seery, if he was the killer, either attempted to destroy incriminating evidence or he didn't. It's as clear as day that this young Irishman, just like his dad, was an innocent victim, legally murdered by the British.

(I) How could saplings exist for about two days after being placed on a blazing fire? The judge, in his summary, stated that, "The fire was so intense it set fire to the timber outside" however, he failed to add that the saplings survived the intense heat from Friday until Sunday, when Constable Coleman arrived at the scene. This begs the question, did some other person put saplings on the blaze for a second time? If so, who was this person? We know Seery was miles away.

Execution of James Seery

His Excellency, the Governor decided that James Seery should be put to death on the morning of Monday, 14 November 1870 at 10am, the execution to be carried out at Melbourne Gaol.

James, right up to his execution, thought it would not take place. He really believed that he would be reprieved. Unfortunately for Seery, the crime of murder and the mutilation of a body, for which he had been found guilty, were rated at the top end of the scale. There was no chance of a reprieve, whether he was guilty or not. Once the jury found against him, he had to die.

Father Lordan, the Roman Catholic chaplain at the prison, attended to his spiritual needs throughout his time on death row. Seery passed his last night on earth in a peaceful manner – he actually slept through most of the night.

At the appointed time, Mr Ellis, the acting sheriff, arrived at the prison and requested the body of the condemned man from the governor, Mr Caslieau. Seery was then removed from his cell and brought to the scaffold. On his way to the drop, a number of the spectators were expecting Seery to show signs of fear and maybe cause a scene. However, he showed no signs of cracking up and behaved with great calmness throughout.

When he arrived at the drop, Mr Bamford, the hangman immediately pinioned his arms behind his back. At this time Father Lordan was reciting prayers, Seery kept his eyes glued on a crucifix held by the chaplain's assistant. Before the lever was pulled, he kissed the crucifix, which of course was the last thing he saw and kissed on this earth. The hangman's assistant then pulled a hood over his head. Bamford, the hangman, placed and adjusted the noose around his neck then, quickly pulled the lever and Seery was launched into eternity. The spectators believed death was instantaneous and that Seery felt no pain, as not a single muscle of his entire body twitched. James, just like his dad, was sent to an early grave under very suspicious circumstances.

It's my opinion, in the Ireland and indeed, Australia of today, neither case would get into court. The British authorities engaged in what I would call "Jungle Justice" – the law of the lion and, we all know the lion is king of the jungle. This animal, like the British, enforces his own justice as he hunts his prey. The unfortunate inhabitants of the jungle, just like the Seerys and thousands like them at that time, were at the mercy of the predator. I can see now why the British adopted the lion (make that three lions) as a symbol of their "greatness": they took on board this animal's approach to life and acted accordingly.

Chapter 13

Who Was James Seery?

James Seery was thirty-three years of age when he was executed by the British in Melbourne Australia. He was the son of Brian Seery, the unfortunate man who was executed by the British in 1846, outside Mullingar Gaol.

At the time of his father's death, James was an ordinary nine-year-old boy, like any other child growing up in Ireland at that time. He got up to all sorts of devilment with his friends who resided in the Brewery Yard/Patrick Street area of the town. That was, until his dad was arrested and charged with firing a shot at Sir Francis Hopkins. James, his family and every other decent person in the Mullingar area knew full well that his dad was innocent of the crime. As a matter of fact, the entire country, with the exception of the gentry, expected the charges to be withdrawn or thrown out of court. As we now know, this didn't happen and, an innocent man was murdered. All of a sudden, James changed from a nine-year-old boy to an adult and quickly realised that he had to get stuck in and assist his mum come to terms with, what was for her, a horrible ordeal.

The ordinary people of Ireland and Britain donated what they could to assist this lady as she endeavoured to get her life back on track. Mary soon realised she had no other option but to get on with life, as she had children to bring up and this was her number one priority. She opened a small shop in Mount Street (Years later re-named Seery Street in honour of her late husband Brian), and, with the help of her children, made a success of the venture. James and his siblings worked long and hard at the business assisting their mum every day in every way. Thanks to the British gentry, these children lost out on their childhood and, let's face it, every child is and was, at that time, entitled to a childhood. James worked for his mum right up to his early twenties. He also did odd jobs for business people and farmers around the area. These people did their utmost to assist the Seery family, by supporting them at every opportunity.

Twenty-three-year-old James, just like other young men in the Mullingar area, heard numerous stories about Australia and the fortunes that could be made there if a man was prepared to work hard. Working on the goldfields, they believed, was the quickest way to earn the much talked about fortune.

After discussing everything with his mum, he made arrangements to undertake the long journey to this faraway land. He had promised his mother he would return to see her after he earned his fortune however, little did he know what awaited him there. He would never see his beloved mother or Ireland again. Despite working long and hard, his life and dreams were brought to an abrupt end by the old enemy, the British.

James sailed to Australia aboard the ship, *Lightening*, in 1861 and, for a short time he was employed on a ranch. He spent about a year working on the farm before he obtained employment in the goldfields. From then up to the time of his arrest for the murder of Auguste Tepfar, he had worked on all the goldfields in the Gippsland area. On the odd occasion, he worked alone but he mostly worked with mates. From the time he was remanded in custody on the murder charge, he remarked that he hadn't communicated to anyone in Mullingar and the only relative he knew of in the colonies was a cousin in New Zealand. He did not think it worthwhile to communicate with him as, he would read about his predicament in the newspapers. I really believe that James didn't want his mother to know that he, just like his dad, was fighting for his life.

As a child, James witnessed the agony on his mother's face as she struggled to come to terms with the reality of her husband fighting a futile battle against the British and, worse still, battling against a trumped-up charge of attempted murder. James' appearance, according to one newspaper, was

> *... rather prepossessing than otherwise. He was not a person whom anyone would have imagined to be likely to commit such a bloody murder.*

He was in trouble with the police before and received a three months' sentence for assault. Seery, on account of the assault charge, was deemed by the police to be insane but, the medical people certified him to be normal and ordered his release.

Incidentally, James' mother was alive and well at the time of his execution. She passed away on 30 October 1906, thirty-six years after his untimely death. However, I don't believe she knew anything about his execution. I say this because his name is not mentioned on the family headstone, located at the old cemetery, Castletown-Geoghegan, Co. Westmeath. On the other hand, the lady could have known about his execution but knew nothing about the case itself and as such, decided not to highlight the event. His mother, Mary (née Gavan), hailed from Crossdrum, Oldcastle, Co. Meath. She probably has relatives residing there to this day.

As I was researching the Brian Seery story, local Mullingar man, John Nooney, called to see me and mentioned the fact that Brian's son, James, was executed in Australia by the British. John handed me old documents containing information about his execution. This news came as a bit of a shock and I immediately realised that I had no other option but to research the James Seery story. In order to discover what really happened in Australia all these years ago, I required the court and newspaper reports in order to establish if he was innocent or guilty. I needed to know everything about the victim and the circumstances surrounding Seery's arrest, conviction and execution.

During my research into the circumstances surrounding the death of James, I spoke with numerous people from the Mullingar/Dysart area. I'm talking about elderly people whose grandparents and great grandparents resided in Dysart and the Brewery Yard/Patrick Street area of Mullingar: not one person knew anything about James' execution. However, I kept going and during my research, I'm happy to say that I discovered the relevant information into what exactly took place in the mining village of Crooked River, Gippsland, Australia in 1870.

James was buried in an unmarked grave in Melbourne prison yard however, during renovations in the 1920s, a number of graves were disturbed and moved elsewhere. I know Ned Kelly's grave was disturbed at that time but, I don't know if Seery's grave was interfered with.

ACKNOWLEDGEMENTS

I am grateful to Gregory O'Connor and Aideen Ireland of the National Archives, Bishop Street, Dublin for their assistance and for permitting the publication of original documents in relation to the Brian Seery case.

I am also grateful to the Irish Newspaper Archives; Cailin Gallagher, Westmeath County Executive Librarian; Gretta Connell, Senior Westmeath County Library Assistant and all the staff in the Westmeath County Library for their assistance.

I would also like to thank the people of Mullingar and Dysart who assisted me as I researched the awful events that afflicted the Seery family in nineteenth century Ireland and Australia. Many thanks to my sisters: Maura (Clara, Co. Offaly) and Ann (Canada); brothers: Tommy (Leixlip), Frankie (Dublin), Paul (Mullingar) and Mick (Canada).

Members of the Kiernan family (relatives of the Seery's) from Rathdrishogue, Dysart, including Jimmy, Declan, Pat and the late Frankie.

Jim Bourke, Mullingar Autos; P.J. Boyle, Mullingar; John Nooney, Mullingar; Dave Charleston, "Gippsland in Picture" for his assistance and brilliant pictures of Gippsland Goldfields, Australia.

I am indebted to my publisher, Oscar Duggan of The Manuscript Publisher, Dublin for his interest and ideas as we prepared the manuscript for publication.

A sincere thanks to my wife, June and my children – Jackie, Marty, Kenny, Lorraine and Paul – for their assistance and patience as I pestered them for nearly two years. Thank you all for listening.

Finally, a big thank you to my sponsor, Kenny Kiernan Carpentry and Building, Mullingar. Ph: 087-6733846 or e-Mail: kennykiernan08@gmail.com

Also by Jack Kiernan

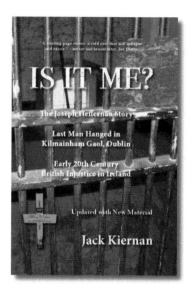

Is It Me? the Joseph Heffernan Story

Published: 2013. **ISBN**: 978-0-9576729-0-1

The murder of Mary Walker, which happened on a warm July day in Mullingar, in 1909, shocked the nation. Joseph Heffernan was subsequently tried and convicted of the crime, receiving the death sentence that would make him the last man to hang in Dublin's notorious Kilmainham Gaol. But there have always been rumours and whispers that Heffernan was simply in the wrong place at the wrong time.

When Jack Kiernan decided to investigate, he discovered a number of strange anomalies and inconsistencies.

A riveting page-turner. ... By the end, the reader is left in no doubt that beautiful young Mary Walker was the victim of a heinous crime, but that crime claimed another life the day Joe Heffernan fell to the hangman's rope.
– **Joe Duffy**, author and broadcaster

Available to Buy Online, in print and e-book editions
For further information, please visit:

www.JackKiernanAuthor.com

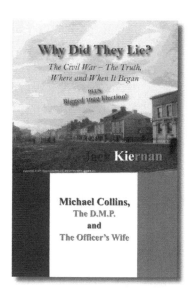

Why Did They Lie?

The Irish Civil War, The Truth, Where and When it Began

Published: 2018. ISBN: 978-1-911442-08-0

Where and when did the Irish Civil War begin? Most people, with any knowledge of Irish history, will tell you that hostilities commenced with the sacking of the Four Courts in Dublin, towards the end of June 1922. However, most people would be wrong! That is the view of Jack Kiernan, who sets out to investigate the roots of a tragic and bitter conflict, that proceeded apace with the emergence of independent Irish statehood.

Part historical investigation, part polemic, he uncovers important events of, not just local but national significance that took place in the midland's town of Mullingar, where he grew up. He also offers an assessment that challenges certain assumptions about the course of events, the personalities and leadership dynamics involved in a conflict that itself took place against the backdrop of a very turbulent period of Irish history.

This book sheds important light on a dark chapter in Irish history.

Available to Buy Online, in print and e-book editions
For further information, please visit:

www.JackKiernanAuthor.com